Beginner's Guide to
Interfacing the BBC Microcomputer

Macmillan Microcomputer Books

General Editor: Ian Birnbaum
(General Adviser (Microelectronics in Education)
Education Department, Humberside County Council))

Advanced Graphics with the Acorn Electron
  Ian O. Angell and Brian J. Jones
Advanced Graphics with the BBC Model B Microcomputer
  Ian O. Angell and Brian J. Jones
Interfacing the BBC Microcomputer
  Brian Bannister and Michael Whitehead
Assembly Language Programming for the Acorn Electron
  Ian Birnbaum
Assembly Language Programming for the BBC Microcomputer (second edition)
  Ian Birnbaum
Using Your Home Computer (Practical Projects for the Micro Owner)
  Garth W. P. Davies
Microchild – Learning through LOGO
  Serafim Gascoigne
The Purple Planet – Micro-PROLOG for the Spectrum 48K
  Serafim Gascoigne
Turtle Fun – LOGO for the Spectrum 48K
  Serafim Gascoigne
A Science Teacher's Companion to the BBC Microcomputer
  Philip Hawthorne
Operating the BBC Microcomputer – A Concise Guide
  Graham Leah
Sorting Routines for Microcomputers
  Keith McLuckie and Angus Barber
Beginning BASIC with the ZX Spectrum
  Judith Miller
Using Sound and Speech on the BBC Microcomputer
  Martin Phillips
File Handling on the BBC Microcomputer
  Brian J. Townsend
Good BASIC Programming on the BBC Microcomputer
  Margaret White

Other Books of related interest

Advanced Graphics with the IBM Personal Computer
  Ian O. Angell
Advanced Graphics with the Sinclair ZX Spectrum
  Ian O. Angell and Brian J. Jones
Micro-Maths
  Keith Devlin
Beginning BASIC
  Peter Gosling
Continuing BASIC
  Peter Gosling
Practical BASIC Programming
  Peter Gosling
Program Your Microcomputer in BASIC
  Peter Gosling
More Real Applications for the ZX81 and ZX Spectrum
  Randle Hurley
The Commodore 64 in Action
  M. M. Novak
Computer Literacy: A beginners' guide
  Vincent Walsh

Beginner's Guide
to
Interfacing
the
BBC Microcomputer

Martin Phillips

MACMILLAN

First published 1985

Published by
MACMILLAN EDUCATION LTD
Houndmills, Basingstoke, Hampshire RG21 2XS
and London
Companies and representatives
throughout the world

Printed in Great Britain by
Camelot Press Ltd

British Library Cataloguing in Publication Data
Phillips, M.A. (Martin A.)
Beginner's guide to interfacing the BBC
Microcomputer.—(Macmillan microcomputer books).
1. Computer interfaces   2. BBC Microcomputer
I. Title
001.64′04   TK7887.5
ISBN 0–333–38652–3

Contents

Preface

One of the most exciting features of the BBC
microcomputer is the range of input and output
facilities that it provides. This makes the BBC
microcomputer an ideal machine for control use. This
book deals with just two of the ports on the BBC, the
User Port and the Analogue Port. It examines the way
that they can be used, shows how devices can be
connected to them, and explains how these devices can
be used in practical applications. It is a beginner's
book. It assumes some knowledge of programming but
little knowledge of electronics. It steers clear of
detailed theory, and concentrates on the practical use
of the two ports.

I am aware that many think that the use of a
soldering iron is beyond them. Soldering is an art, but
a relatively simple art that comes with practice. Every
effort has been made to keep the constructional
projects simple, so that soldering is kept to a
minimum. Another worry is the probability of doing
permanent damage to the computer. The computer is quite
robust, and care has been taken in this book to ensure
that there is as little chance of causing damage to the
computer as possible. Projects that require the use of
the mains or high voltages have been avoided for this
reason, and for reasons of safety. To assist the
beginner, some of the projects are provided with
computer programs that show the sequence of assembly
step-by-step.

I would like to thank Acorn Computers for permission
to reproduce the User Port circuit diagram. I would
also like to thank my son Stuart for the loan of his
Lego. Lastly I would like to thank my wife for her
patience and understanding while this book was being
written.

Martin Phillips

Introduction

Many owners of a BBC microcomputer wish to know how the computer can be used to control external devices. The BBC model B has several ports that can be used to input or output information, and it is an ideal computer for control work. The difficult part is knowing how or where to start. This book assumes that the reader has little knowledge of electronics but some knowledge of BASIC programming, and assumes that the reader will also wish to pick up general programming skills and not just those relating specifically to control applications. Indeed it is difficult to identify a clear border between general programming skills and those programming skills required for control. It is also necessary to have the courage to be adventurous and to experiment, because it is only by building some of the devices that one can appreciate that control can be quite easy.

There are two approaches to the investigation of control applications. One can be presented with a board which simply plugs into one or more of the ports on the BBC micro and provides a medium for inputting from, and outputting to, a variety of devices present on the board. Often the board comes with a set of programs, so that each device can be shown in operation. One needs little skill or understanding to see how such a board works, but extending the principles to practical systems is a difficult gulf to bridge. In this book I have adopted a different approach. Rather than having one board with all the devices displayed and ready to work, this book will examine a series of devices in turn and show how each can be connected to the computer and programmed. It is therefore necessary to have some knowledge of electronic components and electronic assembly techniques. In my experience it is this step that many find difficult. However, that difficulty is more a fear of the unknown, coupled with worry about the serious damage that could be caused by inexperienced hands. After building some of the projects, the reader will become aware that modern electronic components are remarkably robust. Electronic assembly techniques are far from difficult, but as in many other fields their simplicity is often not appreciated until the correct procedures have been learnt and practised. Once all the individual techniques have been developed, and a series of devices examined, then the user has all the skills at his or her fingertips to explore the fascinating world of control, without being constrained by the practical difficulties of building devices. The integration of Lego building techniques in the latter part of the book allows the reader to construct a wide variety of control application models simply and effectively.

This approach has several distinct advantages. It takes much of the mystique out of electronics, and it offers the reader the confidence to explore the world of control beyond the boundaries of purpose-built demonstration boards. It can also help to improve programming skills, and is a much cheaper and infinitely more flexible approach than using commercial boards. Above all, it is open-ended. Having read and digested the contents of the book, the reader has not come to the end of the exploration, but has really just arrived at the starting point - the point where his or her own ideas can be put into practice.

Several projects will be developed within the book to show specific applications of control. The criterion for including such projects is that they should first and foremost be useful, and not result in something that once the novelty has worn off will get consigned to the bottom of the junk box. Such projects must also be inexpensive. Computing is already an expensive hobby without having to incur additional large costs in order to study control applications. Software is important and these projects will require good software to enhance their usefulness and their accuracy. Computer control is an integration of hardware devices and computer software. Some of these projects will be of the 'stand alone' variety, but others can be used with other projects in the book and eventually can be used to make a variety of models that rely on computer control. Above all it is hoped to show the simple concepts that underlie computer control, and to show practical electronic constructional techniques.

Hints on Entering Programs

A great deal can be learned about programming just by typing in listings. In this book there are many short listings and several longer ones too, all of which will be found useful for a better understanding of BBC BASIC. There is nothing worse than typing a program

into the computer only to find that it will   not   work,
so   at   this   stage some tips on typing in the programs
are appropriate.

1. In many programs there are line   numbers   typed   in
    with   just   a colon (:) to follow them.   These have
    been put into the program to break the program down
    into more recognisable   sections.   For   instance   a
    line   with   just   a   colon has always been inserted
    before   a   procedure   is   defined.   This   makes
    identifying   the   procedures that much easier. Such
    lines can be missed out but   to   the   detriment   of
    readability.
2. Some   of   the   programs   have an "ON ERROR GOTO..."
    line. It is better not to put this   line   in   while
    typing in the program; wait until the program works
    correctly.   If   a   typing   mistake is made and this
    line   is   present,   the   program will   not   work
    correctly when run, but will usually go back to the
    start   of   the   program   again   without listing the
    fault. It then often appears that the   program   has
    crashed   completely. You might find that the ESCAPE
    key does not function as it should, however,   until
    this line is inserted.
3. Many   of the DATA lines in programs have been split
    up into short sets of data. This has been   done   to
    avoid confusion when data is being entered.
4. Instead   of   having   large   gaps   between quotes on
    print statements for spaces, the command SPC( ) has
    been used. In many of the programs screen layout is
    critical, and mistakes here cause endless problems.
5. It is useful to program the BREAK key   when   typing
    in listings so that the program cannot be destroyed
    that way. The following line will program the BREAK
    key   to   return to mode 7 and list the program with
    page mode on

            *KEY10 OLD¦M ¦N LIST¦M

    It can be added as line 1 of the program   or   typed
    in as a direct command.
6. Many   of   the   programs   mix   upper   and lower case
    lettering. To avoid taking the CAPS LOCK   off   each
    time,   on   machines fitted with 1.2 OS, if the CAPS
    LOCK is put on while the SHIFT key is pressed, then
    the action of the shift key is reversed   and   lower
    case   lettering   can   be   obtained   when   SHIFT   is
    pressed.
7. Do take care to insert all   the   punctuation   marks
    correctly.   Some very odd results can happen in the
    VDU statements if commas, for instance,   are   typed

instead of semi-colons. Error messages are not generated here and the faults are obscure and hard to find. Forewarned is forearmed!

8. Following the IF statements, the word THEN has been included for greater clarity. The use of the word THEN is optional on the BBC machine and it can be omitted provided that a space is inserted in its place.

9. Again for greater clarity, spaces have been inserted in some program lines. Unless you are confident about where spaces can be inserted and left out, it is advisable to include them or not as in the listings.

10. Do check a listing carefully when it has been typed in. It is better to check the program in small sections, especially if it is one of the longer programs. It is easy to confuse the capital ´O´ with the number ´0´, and this is one thing to pay particular attention to.

11. All the programs in this book have been designed to work with either disc or cassette. It is advisable to save a copy of the program before you run it, or even part way through a long program. In that way, if anything disastrous does happen you always have a copy. You can save incomplete programs or part programs, as well as untested programs, on tape or disc. Time spent in making a copy is often time well spent.

1 Getting Started

This chapter aims to give the reader some knowledge
of the theory of electronics - sufficient to
understand the applications included in the rest of
this book. If readers are thirsty for more detailed
knowledge on the subject then it is recommended
that they consult one of the many textbooks on
electronics. Constructional techniques are covered
in some detail as these are seldom to be found in
publications, and yet knowledge here can turn
´tobacco tin´ projects into pieces of
professional-looking equipment. (There was a time
when the amateur electronics magazines published
many projects that used tobacco tins for a box,
with a maze of wiring and components strung
together inside. Fortunately we have moved on far
from this era, and the amateur now has access to
most of the components available in industry, and
can produce quite respectable quality projects.) I
attach considerable importance to correctly and
elegantly made projects. Apart from aesthetic
considerations, a well-made project will not only
last longer but be more reliable, and there is less
likelihood of damaging the computer because
something went wrong with the project.

THE THEORY OF ELECTRONICS

Electronics, as currently practised, is basically a
simple art - a combination of some basic laws,
rules of thumb, and a large bag of tricks.
Mathematics often plays a large part in textbooks
on electronics. In this book every attempt has been
made to keep the mathematics simple enough so as
not to obscure the underlying theories. For those
who dislike even a minimum of mathematics, the
computer can, as we shall see later, be programmed
to perform much of the calculation. One of the main
difficulties with electronics is its rapid rate of
change. In order to perceive and move with such
change it is better not to get too involved in
detailed theory but to be aware of the main

1

concepts of electronics. Electronic components can be seen as a series of building bricks that can be configured in a wide variety of ways to suit a variety of purposes. These building bricks are becoming more complex and more specific in their function, with the result that the standard of performance increases. One way to view electronics is to treat these building bricks as black boxes.

Black-box Theory
The idea of a black box is a box, the contents of which do a specific function, but which cannot be opened for someone to see what is inside. Therefore, we are concerned with what the box does and not how it works. A cassette recorder is a black box: we put a tape in, connect up a power source and are able to hear the sounds coming out, but we have no notion of how the player works, and we do not need to know. There are different levels of black box. One could delve inside the cassette player and identify several parts each of which has its own special function, and each of which would be another black box. This could continue until we ended up with each discrete component identified and its function ascertained.

If a cassette recorder does not function correctly there are several options open to us. First, we can throw it away and buy a new one. This is treating the recorder as a true black box. It is often the cheapest alternative in the long run. Second, we could take it to a dealer who understands how it works and let him repair it. Third, the various functions of the recorder can be identified and the faulty one can be rectified by the owner. This latter alternative poses many problems. We need to have some information to tell us how the recorder was constructed and what parts do what. Then we need to be able to say in which area the fault has developed. Lastly, once the fault has been discovered we need to obtain an exact replacement part and have the ability to replace it. The question I would pose for those who would shun the black-box technique is - does a knowledge of the workings of a cassette recorder necessarily make one a better user of it? It certainly is not essential to have such detailed knowledge. To go into such detail would obscure the real aims of this book, which is to be able to study and appreciate the implications of computer control.

Integrated circuits are best understood in terms

of black-box techniques. We need to know their power requirements, and what to put into them to get some output, but we do not need to worry about what goes on inside the chip. For this reason you will not find any circuit details of what goes on inside an integrated circuit in this book. Some integrated circuits contain several identical black boxes in one. Here it helps to simplify the function of the complete circuit if each building block is identifiable.

Black-box techniques can be used in programming. The program in appendix 1 uses some procedures almost as black boxes. In other words, so long as it is understood how to implement the procedure in a program it does not matter how the procedure works. An example of this is the procedure to draw double-height characters (PROCdouble). The four parameters that follow it define the string of characters to be printed double-height, the X and Y positions, and the colour in which the characters are to be printed. If one wants to delve into the procedure one meets another level of black box. For instance, what does "CALL&FFF1" do? Having discovered what it does, one could open this black box (harder now, because it is enclosed in the operating system) to find out exactly how it is programmed and how it works.

In other words black-box theory lets us have a simple overview of what is going on without becoming too involved in unnecessary detail. With the increasing use of the integrated circuit this approach is becoming more and more attractive.

Voltage and Current
There are two quantities that we need to keep track of in electronic circuits: voltage and current. These are usually changing with time, otherwise nothing interesting is happening in the circuit. Voltage has the symbol ´V´ and the voltage between two points is the cost in energy (the work done) required to move a unit of positive charge from the more negative point (lower potential) to the more positive point (higher potential). Equivalently, it is the energy released when a unit charge moves ´downhill´ from the higher potential to the lower potential. The unit of measurement is the volt. Small voltages are measured in millivolts. One thousand millivolts equal one volt.

Current has the symbol ´I´ and is the rate of flow of electrical charge past a point. The unit of measurement is the ampere, or amp, with currents often being expressed in milliamps. One thousand milliamps equal one amp. By convention, current in a circuit is considered to flow from a more positive point to a more negative point, even though the actual electron flow is in the reverse direction.

It is important to refer to voltage between two point or across two points. Always refer to current through a device or connection in a circuit. To say something like "The voltage through a resistor...." is nonsense. However, we do speak of the voltage at a point in a circuit. This is always understood to mean the voltage between that point and ´ground´, a common point in a circuit that everyone seems to know about. Soon you will too!

Here are some simple rules about current and voltage.

1. The sum of the currents into a point is equal to the sum of the currents out of the point. Hence for a series circuit (figure 1.1) the current is the same everywhere.

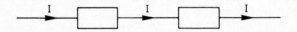

Figure 1.1   A series circuit

2. Things connected in parallel (figure 1.2) have the same voltage across them or, to put it another way, the sum of the ´voltage drops´ from A to B via one path through a circuit equals the sum by any other route and equals the voltage between A and B.

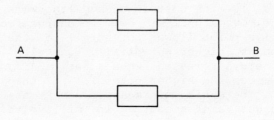

Figure 1.2   A parallel circuit

3. The power (work per unit time) consumed by a circuit
   device is given by

$$P = V \times I$$

The units of power are watts (W). Power often appears
as heat. (Feel the top of the BBC machine after it has
been switched on for a couple of hours.) Power can also
be dissipated as mechanical work as in motors, as sound
in the case of loudspeakers, or as radiated energy in
lamps and transmitters, etc. The heat developed can be
a problem in many circuits and needs some
consideration, especially when components are being
specified.

Relationship Between Voltage and Current

This is the heart of electronics. Crudely speaking, the
name of the game is to make and use gadgets that have
interesting and useful current/voltage characteristics.
Some of these devices will be used in later chapters,
but here we will start with the most mundane (and
widely used) circuit element, the resistor. It is an
interesting fact that the current through a metallic
conductor (or partially conducting material) is
proportional to the voltage across it. (In the case of
wire conductors the wire is chosen so that it is thick
enough to have a negligible voltage drop across it.)
This is by no means a universal law for all objects.
The current through a neon tube is a highly non-linear
function of the applied voltage. The same goes for a
variety of special devices - diodes, transistors, light
bulbs, etc.
   A resistor is made out of some conducting material
(carbon, or thin metal, or carbon film, or wire of poor
conductivity), with a wire coming out at each end. It
usually has coloured bands around it. It is
characterised by its resistance

$$R = \frac{V}{I}$$

R is in ohms, V in volts and I in amps. This is known
as Ohm's Law.

Resistors in Series and Parallel

If two resistors are placed in a circuit so that the
electricity flows first through one and then through
the other, they are said to be wired in series. If they
are wired so that the electricity can flow through both

at once then they are said to be wired in parallel.
   From the definition of resistance, some simple
results follow.

1. The resistance of two resistors in series is

$$R = R_1 + R_2$$

(figure 1.3). By putting two resistors in series,
you always get a larger total value of resistance.

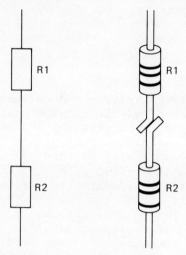

Figure 1.3   Resistors in series

2. The resistance of two resistors in parallel (figure
1.4) is

$$R = \frac{1}{\frac{1}{R_1} + \frac{1}{R_2}}$$

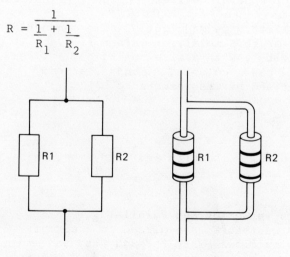

Figure 1.4   Resistors in parallel

By putting resistors in parallel, you always get a smaller value of resistance. Resistance is measured in ohms (Ω), but in practice we frequently omit the Ω symbol when referring to resistors of more than 1000Ω (1 KΩ). Thus a 10 KΩ resistor is often referred to as a 10 K resistor.

Voltage Dividers

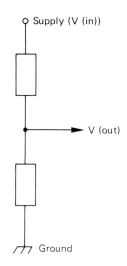

Figure 1.5   A voltage divider circuit

One of the commonest uses of resistors is in voltage divider circuits. This simple circuit is shown in figure 1.5. What is V_{out} ? If there is no load on the output then the current flow through the resistors is the same, and if we know V_{in} and the value of the two resistors, we can calculate V_{out}.

Note that the output voltage cannot be greater than the input voltage, that is why the circuit is called a divider.

Voltage and Current Sources
A perfect voltage source is a two-terminal black box that maintains a fixed voltage drop across the two terminals, regardless of the load resistance. A real voltage source can supply only a finite maximum current, and in addition there is usually a small drop in voltage as the current increases. In most of the applications considered in this book, the current

consumed by the circuit is so small that there is a negligible drop in voltage. The power source could be batteries or, as will be used in this book, the BBC´s own power supply, which converts mains voltage down to a suitable level that is safe to touch. The output of this power supply is also completely isolated from the mains supply for safety reasons. As will be seen in later chapters, the BBC microcomputer is thoughtfully provided with several ways of accessing the power supply.

Computing Simple Circuit Values
Appendix 1 contains the listing of a program that will save time when circuit values are being calculated. It has a series of options that enable the user to perform all the calculations so far introduced.

Components

One only has to study the electronic component catalogues to see the amazing array of devices and bits and pieces used in electronics. To the beginner such a variety of parts can seem daunting. The next part of this chapter deals with those component types that will be used for projects in this book.

Electronic engineers have a form of shorthand when designing circuits. They do not draw each component out in true detail but use circuit symbols. Although there are British Standards on circuit symbols, many variations can be found. Figure 1.6 shows the circuit symbols for some of the components used in this book. The symbols are joined by conductors depicted by straight lines. Where the lines join, there is a visible dot. If there is no dot, the lines are assumed to cross without any connection being made.

The Resistor
Resistors come in a wide variety of sizes and shapes, but they all do the same thing: limit (or resist) current. They are available with resistances from 0.1 ohms through to 10^{12} ohms, with power ratings from 0.1 watt to 250 watts, and accuracies from 0.005% to 20%. The circuit symbol for the resistor is shown in figure 1.6. The commonest type of resistor is the carbon film resistor. It is made by depositing a thin layer of carbon on to a small former which has a lead attached at each end. There are many other types of resistor that can be commonly found. These include the metal film resistor, thick film resistor networks, the wirewound resistor and potentiometers. Generally

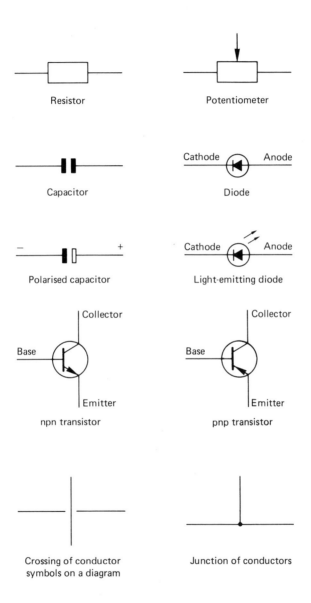

Figure 1.6   Circuit symbols

speaking, metal film resistors are slightly more expensive that carbon film resistors but are made to a closer tolerance (often 1% as opposed to 5%). Also their values are less likely to change with age than those of the carbon film resistors. Thick film resistor networks are becoming more common. These contain up to 8 resistors all in one package. They are often used in computers where it is necessary to connect several leads each through its own resistor to one point in the circuit. Wirewound resistors are used where the resistor will have a large current passing through it. They are made of resistance wire wrapped round a ceramic former, and have a power rating from 3 watts upwards. The carbon film resistor generally has a power rating of about 0.25 watts, which is quite sufficient for the majority of circuit applications.

The type of resistor needed for the projects in this book is generally not critical, a power rating of 0.25 watt (or 0.33 watt) is more than enough. Larger rated resistors offer no advantages, yet are bigger and in consequence more difficult to mount on the circuit board. The only project which is critical as regards the type of resistor used is the multimeter project. Here the consideration is that of resistor accuracy. The more accurate the resistor, the more accurate the final meter. The multimeter also uses a wirewound resistor. This is necessary because in the current-measuring mode, the resistor could have up to 5 amps flowing through it. A 0.25 watt resistor of the required value would overheat at this current.

The majority of electronic components cannot be made with any great accuracy at a price to suit all needs. This means that the ´tolerance´ of the component is important. Resistors are no exception. Ten years ago it was the norm for resistors to have a 20% tolerance; that is, it could be as much as 20% out against the stated value. This could mean a value of 20% greater or 20% less than that stated - 40% difference! Today the common tolerance is 5%, and it is possible to get 1% tolerance resistors at little extra cost. However, one legacy of earlier days remains. When a series of resistors had a 20% tolerance, there was little point in making a great range of values. Therefore for each decade range, it was necessary to have just 12 values. All resistors are available in these values, and because the tolerances have reduced, a further 12 in-between values can be obtained also.

1.0	1.0
	1.1
1.2	1.2
	1.3
1.5	1.5
	1.6
1.8	1.8
	2.0
2.2	2.2
	2.4
2.7	2.7
	3.0
3.3	3.3
	3.6
3.9	3.9
	4.3
4.7	4.7
	5.1
5.6	5.6
	6.2
6.8	6.8
	7.5
8.2	8.2
	9.1

The common decade ranges for carbon film resistors are $10\,\Omega$ to $82\,\Omega$, $100\,\Omega$ to $820\,\Omega$, 1 KΩ to 8.2 KΩ, 10 KΩ to 82 KΩ, and 100 KΩ to 820 KΩ. Wirewound resistors are obtainable in values that go as low as $0.22\,\Omega$, and they seldom go above 10 KΩ. When writing resistor values, the multiplier (R for x1, k or K for x1000 and M for x1000000) is often put in place of the decimal point; for example 2R2, 1K2, 1M0.

As the majority of resistors are just too small to have their value written on them, a system of coloured bands is used to show their value. Just to add to the confusion, either 4 or 5 bands can be used! In fact, the system is not as hard to work out as might at first appear.

Four Band Resistor Code
Three of the bands are close together at one end of the resistor, and the fourth is at the opposite end. The single band should be at the right-hand side for the bands to be read correctly. The first band on the body of the resistor indicates the first figure of the value, the second band the second value. The third band is the amount by which the first two numbers must be multiplied. The fourth band indicates the tolerance.

Colour	Band 1 1st Figure	Band 2 2nd Figure	Band 3 Multiplier	Band 4 Tolerance
Black	0	0	x1	
Brown	1	1	x10	1%
Red	2	2	x100	2%
Orange	3	3	x1000	
Yellow	4	4	x10000	
Green	5	5	x100000	
Blue	6	6	x1000000	
Violet	7	7		
Grey	8	8		
White	9	9		
Gold			x0.1	5%
Silver			x0.01	10%
None				20%

Five Band Resistor Code

Four of the bands are close together at one end of the resistor, and the other is at the opposite end. This too should be at the right-hand side of the resistor as it is read. It is read in a similar way to the four band code.

Colour	Band 1 1st Fig.	Band 2 2nd Fig.	Band 3 3rd Fig.	Band 4 Multiplier	Band 5 Tolerance
Black	0	0	0	x1	
Brown	1	1	1	x10	1%
Red	2	2	2	x100	2%
Orange	3	3	3	x1000	
Yellow	4	4	4	x10000	
Green	5	5	5	x100000	0.5%
Blue	6	6	6	x1000000	0.25%
Violet	7	7	7	x10000000	0.1%
Grey	8	8	8		0.01%
White	9	9	9		
Gold				x0.1	5%
Silver				x0.01	10%

If these colour bands seem difficult to master at first, then turn to appendix 2 where a program is included to help you practise colour band recognition. Also many shops sell resistor colour code calculators which help to identify resistor values.

Variable Resistors

Variable resistors are resistors with a mechanical mechanism which allows the length of the resistance material to be changed, hence changing the resistance. Small variable resistors are normally called potentiometers. There are circuit board mounting types that can be adjusted with a screwdriver, or larger types which have a spindle on to which a knob can be screwed. Some types of potentiometer have straight tracks and these are known as slide potentiometers. Potentiometers of both types are used for volume and tone controls in amplifiers and television sets. Potentiometers are three-lead devices; the graphical symbol used in circuit diagrams is shown in figure 1.6. The tracks are made of a variety of resistive materials, carbon being the cheapest and most common. Wirewound tracks are much more expensive but offer higher current rating, and better linearity; that is, the resistance changes in a more linear fashion with rotation. This latter quality is important if the user wishes to sense the resistance as a measure of the angle turned. The graphics tablet project requires highly linear potentiometers to function accurately.

Capacitors

There are many types of capacitor, but they all do the same thing: store electricity. The simplest capacitor is two conductors separated by an insulating material called a dielectric. The dielectric can be paper, plastic film, mica, glass ceramic or air. The conductor is often a piece of aluminium foil. Capacitors come in an amazing variety of shapes and sizes, as the conductors and dielectric can be either flat, or rolled up or even interleaved like a book. Figure 1.7 shows some of the configurations for small capacitors.

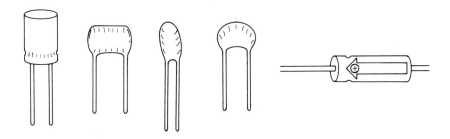

Figure 1.7   Types of capacitors

Each type of capacitor has different properties that can affect a circuit. In general, ceramic and Mylar types are used for most non-critical circuit applications and these are the cheapest; tantalum capacitors are used when a greater capacitance is needed, and electrolytic capacitors are used for power supply filtering. Figure 1.8 compares the different types available. The comments should be considered as rather subjective.

Capacitors are specified by the maximum charge that they can hold. This is measured in farads. Capacitors are rather more complicated than resistors, the current flowing through the capacitor not simply being proportional to the voltage, but rather to the rate of change of voltage. If the voltage across a capacitor is changed by 1 volt per second then 1 amp is supplied. Conversely, if 1 amp is supplied, then the voltage changes by 1 volt per second. A farad is a very large unit of capacitance, and we usually deal in microfarads (μF) or picofarads (pF). A microfarad is one-millionth of a farad, and a picofarad one-millionth of a microfarad.

Type	Capacitance Range	Maximum Voltage	Accuracy	Temperature Stability	Leakage	Comments
Mica	1pF-0.01μF	100-600	Good	Good	Good	Excellent, good for high frequencies
Ceramic	10pF-1μF	50-1000	Poor	Poor	Good	Small and inexpensive
Mylar	0.001μF-10μF	50-600	Good	Poor	Good	Inexpensive, good, very popular
Polystyrene	10pF-0.01μF	100-600	Good	Fair	Excellent	High quality, large
Tantalum	0.1μF-500μF	6-100	Poor	Poor	Poor	High capacitance, small size, expensive, polarised
Electrolytic	0.1μF-0.2μF	3-600	Awful	Terrible	Abysmal	Used for power supply filters, polarised, short shelf-life

Figure 1.8   Comparison of capacitors

The accuracy of capacitors is generally far worse than resistors; one is lucky to find 5% accuracy, usually the accuracy is 20%, or in the case of electrolytic capacitors accuracies are often quoted as -10% +75%! It is possible to get silver mica capacitors with accuracies as good as 1%.

The leakage of a capacitor is the rate at which the charge leaks across the dielectric. One of the worst capacitors here is the electrolytic capacitor, and in many circuits this leakage could have quite an effect on the operation of the circuit. As capacitors are

usually used to ´block´ a direct current and allow only
a varying current to pass, a high leakage capacitor
will often cause the circuit to perform incorrectly.
Fortunately for the constructor of digital circuits,
there is not the same dependence on capacitors as there
is in, say, filter circuits. A small capacitor is often
required across the power line of an integrated circuit
or group of circuits, and this can be a disc ceramic.
It is often worth putting an electrolytic capacitor
across the supply lines on a circuit board, especially
if there are long supply leads. This tends to reduce
the effects of voltage fluctuations caused by sudden
changes in the power requirements.

It is also essential to respect the voltage rating
printed on the case of an electrolytic capacitor, as a
voltage applied across the terminals in excess of the
stated voltage will cause the capacitor to fail.
Electrolytic capacitors also have a short shelf-life;
in time (which can be as short as 2-3 years from the
date of manufacture), the dielectric deteriorates and
the capacitor develops an even higher leakage. This
deterioration occurs only if the capacitor remains
unused for that time span. For this reason it is false
economy to buy ´bargain packs´ of old electrolytic
capacitors.

Similarly the polarity of an electrolytic capacitor
is important. It will fail if connected the wrong way
round. The printed circuit board mounting types are
usually clearly marked, but the axial lead ones are
not. An axial lead capacitor is built into an aluminium
tube with a rubber seal at one end. The wire coming
through this rubber seal is the positive terminal.

Diodes and LEDs
The circuit elements discussed so far (resistors and
capacitors) are linear, meaning that a doubling of the
applied signal produces a doubling of the response. The
diode is a very useful two-terminal, passive,
non-linear device. The circuit diagram of a diode is
shown in figure 1.6. The diode will allow a flow of
current only in one direction, from anode to cathode,
the direction of the current flow being indicated by
the direction of the arrow in the circuit diagram. The
diode is not a perfect conductor; there is a 0.5-0.8
volt drop when the diode is conducting. A LED is a
light-emitting diode. It uses a very small amount of
power yet emits a good light, and so is ideal for use
with low power circuits. LEDs can be obtained in
several colours - red, green, yellow and orange being
the most common. They are frequently used now for level
meters in stereo equipment and for small signal lights.

The graphical symbol used in circuit diagrams for a LED is shown in figure 1.6. As LEDs are actually diodes, it is important to connect them the right way round. The cathode of the LED is usually identified by a small flat on the side of the body and by a short lead.

Transistors
The transistor is the most important example of an ´active´ component, which is a device that can amplify, producing an output signal with more power in it than the input signal. The transistor is the essential ingredient of almost every electronic circuit. Integrated circuits (ICs) which are rapidly replacing circuits constructed from discrete transistors, are themselves merely arrays of transistors and other components built from a single chip of semiconducting material. To explain fully how a transistor works is outside the scope of this book, and the introduction to the transistor given here is both brief and incomplete.

Transistors are three-terminal components. They come packaged in a variety of ways, and these are often detailed in the electronic component catalogues. There are two main sorts of transistor, **npn** and **pnp**. Figure 1.6 shows the circuit diagrams of the two types of transistor. Essentially a **pnp** is a **npn** transistor with the current flows reversed. **npn** transistors are the most widely used.

The following rules apply to the **npn** transistor.

1. The collector must be more positive than the emitter.
2. Currents and voltages outside the ranges specified for that transistor will cause the transistor to fail.
3. The current flowing from collector to emitter divided by the current flowing into the base of the transistor will be the ´gain´ or amplification factor of the transistor. Typically, current gains for small general-purpose transistors are of the order of 30-200.

In an **npn** transistor, the current flows from the collector to the emitter. The amount of current flowing across the transistor depends on the voltage across the transistor and on the base current. The base then acts as a variable switch to limit the current flow.

Digital Integrated Circuits
Digital circuits are circuits in which there are (usually) only two states possible at any point. We

generally choose to talk about voltages rather than
currents, calling a level HIGH or LOW.

There are different 'families' of digital integrated
circuits, each with different characteristics. There
are two main families, these are TTL (transistor-
transistor logic) and CMOS (complementary metal oxide
silicon). There are several manufacturers that make
each of the logic gates in these families. TTL is the
older logic, and requires a supply voltage of 5 volts.
A LOW condition of a TTL logic circuit is less that 0.4
volts, and a HIGH state will be over 2.4 volts. The
threshold is generally about 1.4 volts. CMOS logic
requires a supply voltage from +5 volts to +15 volts.
The threshold depends on the supply voltage and can
vary between one-third and two-thirds of the supply
voltage. TTL logic is faster than CMOS, whereas CMOS
requires less power. TTL logic is used for the
applications in this book, mainly because it can sink a
far greater current than can CMOS logic. The only logic
gate that will be used in this book is the NAND gate.
Figure 1.9 shows the circuit symbol and the truth table
for the NAND gate. If a gate is unused, then the gate
should be tied to the supply line through a resistor.

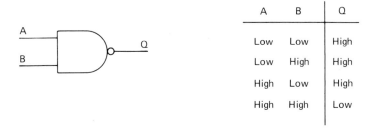

A	B	Q
Low	Low	High
Low	High	High
High	Low	High
High	High	Low

Figure 1.9   The NAND gate

It is important to fit the integrated circuit the
right way round in the circuit. With the pins pointing
down, and the small notch at one end pointing to the
top, the pin to the left of the notch is pin 1. One
trap for the beginner is to forget that when a circuit
is turned upside down then the connections appear
reversed. Although the logic gates are as cheap as the
integrated circuit sockets, it is always wise to use

sockets. In that way there is no danger of damaging the IC when soldering, or of having the problem of removing a chip should the circuit be damaged.

If it is necessary to unsolder a damaged chip, then cut all the pins first, and unsolder each remaining leg in turn. Trying to unsolder 14 or 16 pins at once is not possible without special tools, and one is likely to damage the circuit board.

Techniques

The two things that may put many people off do-it-yourself projects to interface to a computer are the fear of doing irreparable damage to the computer and the thought of soldering. Provided that no voltages greater than +5 volts are used, and reasonable care is taken, there is little chance of damaging the computer. All the projects in this book rely on the power provided by the computer itself, in order to reduce the danger of damage to the computer.

The other worry is a fear of soldering. Good-quality tools and plenty of practice can soon overcome this fear. The construction techniques have been kept as straightforward as possible, and there is plenty of scope for ´packaging´ many of the projects to give a pleasing appearance.

How to solder

The first step to good soldering is a good soldering iron. A solder gun is not recommended, nor is the old ´electric poker´ type soldering iron that has been in the family for generations. Small lightweight soldering irons can be bought in the shops quite cheaply. The best ones to buy have replaceable iron-clad bits which simply slide over the element. Such bits do not need filing, and can be cleaned by wiping on a damp sponge. Also essential is a good soldering iron stand as soldering irons get very hot, and accidents are easily caused when the iron is left propped at the edge of a bench or table. The stand should have a small sponge for cleaning the bit in the base. Always make sure that the power lead is out of the way and that no one can trip over it.

Always use solder with a non-corrosive flux, not acid-cored solder; 22 SWG is an ideal gauge to use, and does not put too much solder on the joint at any one time. Make sure that the components to be soldered are clean, dry and grease-free. Solder will not adhere to dirty or tarnished surfaces. If necessary clean the surfaces with fine wire wool, but do this with care. (Veroboard tends to tarnish and is often easier to

solder if it is gently cleaned before the components
are inserted and soldered.) To solder, first heat both
the connections for a few seconds, then apply the
solder to the joint. When the solder has flowed and
formed an even joint remove the iron, keeping the joint
still. When the joint cools it should have a shiny
surface, and the solder should have flowed evenly round
the connection. Do not be too afraid of damaging the
components with heat; more problems are caused by not
having the connections hot enough before soldering. Do
not apply too much solder. The joint should be slightly
concave, rather than convex. When soldering to the
Veroboard, take care not to bridge two adjacent copper
tracks with solder. This is where a soldering iron with
a fine bit is needed.

   If soldering wires to a plug, first ensure that the
plug is firmly held in a clamp or small vice, otherwise
one ends up chasing it round the bench with the
soldering iron. Failing a clamp or vice, Sellotape or
Plasticine can be used to hold it down. Next strip the
ends of the wire; about 5 mm is sufficient for a wire
that is to be soldered to a plug. Twist the strands of
wire together (resist the temptation to use solid core
wire, it breaks too quickly), and then ´tin´ the wire.
Tinning is done by heating the end of the wire, then
applying a little solder so that it runs between the
strands and forms a solid wire. This is a good gauge of
one´s soldering ability. With practice one should be
able to do this without burning the insulation, or
without leaving a great blob of solder on the end. Then
tin the terminals on the socket and, with a little
solder on the tip of the iron, solder the wire to the
terminal. There should be no need to apply any more
solder; in any case this is rather difficult to do
unless one has three hands.

   To make soldering easier, whenever possible make
sure that the wire or component to be soldered is first
mechanically fastened. If soldering a wire to a tag on
a potentiometer, bend the wire through the hole in the
tag, or wrap it around the tag and squeeze it tight
with fine-pointed pliers. If fitting a component to a
circuit board, then bend the leads slightly so that the
component cannot fall out. If soldering an integrated
circuit socket, bend the opposite corner pins out to
hold the socket in place.

Using Veroboard

Veroboard is Paxolin board that has holes drilled in it
0.1 inch apart. One side of the board has copper strips
which link the holes in strips running the full length
of the board. The pitch of 0.1 inch is the same pitch

that integrated circuits have, so that they will simply
drop into position on the board. Veroboard is easy to
obtain from a variety of sources. It can be cut by
sawing along the lines of holes with a Junior hacksaw
and then filing the edges smooth. The copper tracks can
be cut with a special spot-face cutter. If one's budget
for tools is running low, then a 3.5 mm drill bit held
between the fingers is quite sufficient to drill
through the thin copper track. To cut the track, put
the cutter in a hole on the copper side of the board
and drill through the board until the copper track has
been severed. It is not necessary, nor desirable, to
drill right through the board. All the circuits in this
book have been designed and built using Veroboard. This
is far easier to use than, say, making one's own
circuit boards. This is a tedious and time-consuming
task, and it is not very easy to make the boards
accurately enough for integrated circuit sockets to
fit.

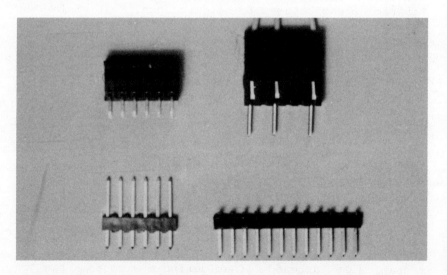

Figure 1.10   The Minicon connection system

There is a convenient and cheap connection system
that can be used with Veroboard, either to link two or
more boards together or to link wires to the board.
This system is known under several names, but is a
miniature 0.1 inch pitched system that fits into the
Veroboard with no extra drilling. Maplin (see the list
of suppliers at the end of the chapter) call it the
Minicon system, Farnell call it KK connectors and RS
Components simply call it the inter-PCB connection
system. The system consists of plugs which are a series
of pins linked by a small plastic strip (see figure

1.10). The plugs can be either straight or right-angled. The sockets fit on the end of the Veroboard, and mate with the plug. Free sockets are also available so that wires can simply be plugged in. Polarising pins are also available for the sockets, so that if the appropriate pin of the plug is cut off or removed before soldering, then there is no possibility that the plug can be connected the wrong way round. Although this connection system is used in several projects, wrong connections are avoided by changing the position of the polarising key.

A Minimum Toolkit
The tools suggested below should be seen as an essential minimum kit to build the majority of projects in this book.

        Miniature soldering iron 18-25 Watt
        Soldering iron stand
        22 SWG solder
        Side-cutting pliers
        Snipe-nosed pliers
        Wire strippers
        Junior hacksaw
        3.5 mm drill bit
        (Veroboard spot-face cutter)
        Fine file, or fine glass-paper
        Small flat-bladed screwdriver
        Modeller´s craft knife

Suppliers
All the projects in this book have been designed with a minimum of special components. Most of the components can be obtained from a variety of sources. One of the better suppliers for the hobbyist is Maplin. Their catalogue is available in leading booksellers, and their service is good.

Farnell Electronic Components and RS Components do not usually deal with the hobby market, but your local electronics supply shop should be able to order the few special components that will be required should they not stock them. Other suppliers can be found by looking at the advertisments in electronics magazines.

        Maplin Electronic Supplies
        PO Box 3
        Rayleigh
        Essex
        SS6 8LR

RS Components
PO Box 99
Corby
Northants
NN17 9RS

Farnell Electronic Components Ltd
Canal Road
Leeds
LS12 2TU

2 The User Port

The User Port on the BBC microcomputer (figure 2.1) is situated underneath the computer keyboard in the middle of a row of multi-way sockets. It is an 8-bit, two-way digital port. That is to say it can handle eight separate digital signals at any one time. These signals can be configured so that information is sent into the computer from external devices, or can be configured to send signals out from the computer to other digital devices. The User Port is connected inside the computer to a very complex chip, a 6522 Versatile Interface Adaptor (VIA) chip. The 6522 VIA not only handles the eight separate data lines of the User Port, but also controls the parallel Printer Port as well. It has two timers built into it. These can be used for timing very short time-intervals. The use of these is outside the scope of this book. There are two 6522 VIA chips inside the BBC machine, VIA A and VIA B. VIA A handles some functions from the Analogue Port, the keyboard input, and the serial input/output through the speech processor. VIA B handles the User and Printer Ports.

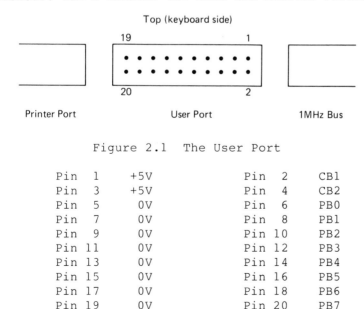

Figure 2.1   The User Port

Pin	1	+5V		Pin	2	CB1
Pin	3	+5V		Pin	4	CB2
Pin	5	0V		Pin	6	PB0
Pin	7	0V		Pin	8	PB1
Pin	9	0V		Pin	10	PB2
Pin	11	0V		Pin	12	PB3
Pin	13	0V		Pin	14	PB4
Pin	15	0V		Pin	16	PB5
Pin	17	0V		Pin	18	PB6
Pin	19	0V		Pin	20	PB7

PB0 to PB7 are the 8 signal lines, CB1 and CB2 are two control lines which are useful for passing 'handshaking' signals between the computer and the peripheral devices.

THE 6522 VIA

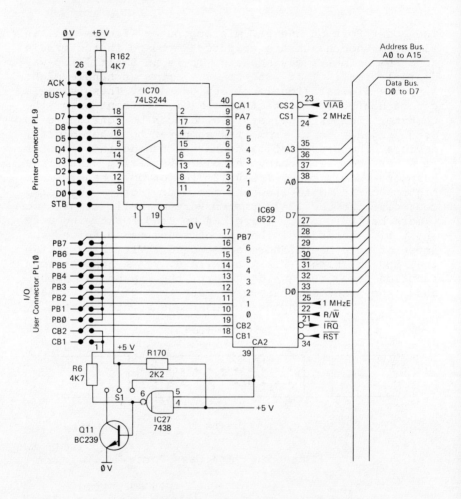

Figure 2.2   The Printer and User Port wiring diagram

The 6522 VIA (see figure 2.2) contains two 8-bit bidirectional input/output ports, two 16-bit timer/counters, and is TTL-compatible. One of the 8-bit bidirectional input/output ports, Port A, is used as the parallel printer output and is connected to the parallel printer socket through a 74LS244 octal buffer/line driver chip. Port B is connected directly

to the User Port. Were it not for the 74LS244 buffer
chip, it would be possible to use the parallel Printer
Port in exactly the same way as the User Port. As it
is, the Printer Port could be programmed to act as an
8-bit output port only. As the Printer Port has a
different sized socket and different connections to the
User Port, no practical use will be made of it for the
purposes of control. Nor need its programming be
considered, as it has already been programmed by the
operating system, and information can simply be sent
out of the port by first using any of the enable
printer commands (VDU2, PRINT CHR$(2), or by pressing
CTRL-B).

The User Port is not so simple to use. Port B of the
6522 VIA first has to be configured for input or for
output. Then information has to be directed through the
6522 to the User Port.

The 6522 has 16 internal registers. The VIA can be
programmed by writing to these registers.

Register Number	Register Name	Function
0	ORB/IRB	Input/Output Register B
1	ORA/IRA	Input/Output Register A
2	DDRB	Data Direction Register B
3	DDRA	Data Direction Register A
4	T1C-L	Timer 1, Low-Order Counter/Latches
5	T1C-H	Timer 1, High-Order Counter
6	T1L-L	Timer 1, Low-Order Latches
7	T1L-H	Timer 1, High-Order Latches
8	T2C-L	Timer 2, Low-Order Counter/Latches
9	T2C-H	Timer 2, High-Order Counter
10	SR	Shift Register
11	ACR	Auxiliary Control Register
12	PCR	Peripheral Control Register
13	IFR	Interrupt Flag Register
14	IER	Interrupt Enable Register
15	ORA/IRA	As reg 1, but no ´handshaking´

In the BBC computer, register 0 is situated at
memory location &FE60, register 1 at memory location
&FE61, etc. The easiest way to program the User Port is
to ´poke´ a number into the appropriate memory
location. This means that a number is directly inserted
into that memory location. This is a process that is
normally shunned in the BBC microcomputer as it will
not work if a second processor is connected, but
surprisingly enough there is no easy way of programming

the User Port with BASIC statements in the same way as the Analogue Port can be read with the ADVAL statement. Hence programming the User Port tends to look ´messy´, and such programs are not easy to follow without plenty of REM statements to indicate what is being done.

To program port B as an output port, it is necessary to write to Data Direction Register B (DDRB). If one bit of this register is set to 0, then the corresponding bit of Port B will be set to input. If the one bit of DDRB is set to 1, then the corresponding bit of Port B will be set to output. DDRB has 8 bits, each corresponding to one bit of port B. The following table shows how each bit is set and cleared.

Port B	DDRB set for Input	DDRB set for Output
PB0	0	1
PB1	0	2
PB2	0	4
PB3	0	8
PB4	0	16
PB5	0	32
PB6	0	64
PB7	0	128

Therefore to set PB0 to output, it is necessary to poke location &FE62 with the value 1. The BBC computer has a rather unusual way of peeking (looking at a memory location) and poking (altering a memory location). This is done by using the ´?´ for both operations and the computer decides which it is to be from the context of the statement. To poke location &FE62 with the value of 1, the following would have to be typed in

        ?&FE62=1

The ´?´ is used as a byte indirection operator. (A byte is a set of 8 bits.) This allows the user to read from, and write to memory locations in a far more flexible way than by using the PEEK and POKE statements which are available in many other versions of BASIC, but not in BBC BASIC. To set PB0-PB3 to output it is necessary to poke a value of 15 (1+2+4+8) into location &FE62. To write a value to the User Port itself, location &FE60 needs to be poked

        ?&FE60=value

Similarly this location needs to be peeked to look at
the value that is being input

        value=?&FE&0

If all this seems rather too much to cope with at once,
it becomes much easier when it is possible to
experiment with the User Port and actually see the
effect.
    Each input will accept a voltage between 0 volts and
5 volts. Voltages greater that 5 volts will damage the
chip. The input will be on if the input voltage is
greater than 2.4 volts, and will be off if the input
voltage is less than 0.4 volts. Set to output, each
line will source a current of 1.4 mA, and provide a
voltage of greater than 2.4 volts (typically over 3
volts) when at a logic state 1, and under 0.4 volts
when at logic state 0.

CONNECTING THE USER PORT
The User Port is a 20-pin IDC socket. IDC stands for
Insulation Displacement Connector. This is a clever
system for quickly and simply linking a large number of
connections without soldering. The connections are
strong and reliable. For the experimenter there is one
disadvantage, that is cost. IDC connectors are not
cheap and if a large number have to be bought, it can
work out rather expensive. The first construction
project then is a simple board to bring out the pins of
the User Port to a cheaper terminal system so that a
variety of devices can be built and tested without the
expense of an IDC plug and ribbon cable each time.
    One thing that puts many people off attempting such
projects is the fear of wiring up a project incorrectly
and causing extensive damage to the computer. About the
worst damage that could be caused by such a mistake is
that the 6522 VIA is blown. This costs a little over £4
to replace (at the time of writing), and is fitted in a
socket on the BBC microcomputer´s main circuit board.
Using most of the devices, there is little chance of
damage even if the project is incorrectly wired, but if
a power supply of more than 5 volts is used or one is
using electric motors or relays there is a greater risk
of damage. It is best to ignore the worry of damage to
the computer, and to accept that, if the worst comes to
the worst, a new 6522 VIA will have to be bought. This
is readily available, but seldom needed.
    The system of boards is so designed that new devices
can be quickly and simply connected to the computer
with little fear of incorrectly linking the devices to
the board. Also, cost has been borne in mind and the

system, although professional looking, is cheap to build and extend; it only uses parts that can be easily obtained from a variety of sources.

The idea of the system is a 'link board' which is connected directly to the User Port socket. This board then has the main connections brought out to a 12-way socket. It is then possible to plug a variety of modules to the link board to provide several functions. This chapter will show how to build and use the link board, a switched input board, and an output board with LED indicators. Chapter 3 will develop some User Port applications to show how other devices and systems can be used and programmed.

THE LINK BOARD
The link board is a small circuit board which is connected to the User Port; it has a 12-way socket carrying +5 volts from the computer, a 0 volt line, PB0-PB7, CB1 and CB2. The latter two connections will be described in chapter 3.

Components required

1	20-way dual-in-line IDC connector
1 metre	20-way IDC cable
1 piece	0.1 Veroboard, 34 tracks by 26 holes
1	12-way Minicon socket (right-angled)
2	Cable clamping strips
2	3 mm nuts and screws

Construction
First check the IDC ribbon cable. It is important to get the right cable. Some ribbon cables are not quite the right size and do not connect up properly. The cable can be checked by laying the end in the grooves on the IDC connector. If a 20-way cable cannot be obtained, it is possible to buy a wider cable and strip off the excess wires. These cables will usually tear lengthwise, quite readily. The IDC connectors are sometimes fitted with small keys so that they will fit only one way round in the User Port socket. This should be checked so that the wire can be fitted from the right side of the connector.

No wire stripping is needed to connect the cable to the IDC connector. The cable must be positioned carefully in the grooves of the connector and the top part clamped over until it locks into place. This requires quite a lot of pressure, and it is best to clamp it in a vice. The short length of wire sticking out of one side of the connector can be trimmed level

with the connector using a sharp knife. Do remember to
cut away from your fingers! Next cut a piece of
Veroboard so that it is 34 tracks wide and the tracks
are 25 holes long. It should be cut with a fine hacksaw
and the edges filed smooth. Check that none of the cut
edges of the copper track short out at the edges of the
board.

The 20-way IDC cable has thin copper conductors, and
it is necessary to clamp the cable securely to the
board to avoid them breaking. It is well worth making a
strong secure clamp otherwise one can be plagued with
broken leads. The clamp for this board (figure 2.3)
consists of two pieces of steel screwed either side of
the Veroboard, trapping the cable and holding it firmly
against the board. The two strips of steel are each 6
cm long by 1 cm wide and 2 mm thick. A 3.5 mm diameter
hole is drilled 7 mm from each end of the strips.

Before starting construction there are two points to
take careful note of. The first is the ´side´ of the
Veroboard. It has two sides, the component side (that
is the plain Paxolin side) and the track side (that is
the side with the copper strips on it). The
descriptions and pictures in this book, such as figure
2.4, all refer to the component side, and these
positions will have to be reversed when working on the
track side. The second point concerns co-ordinates. To
simplify construction, as well as diagrams of the
circuit board layouts, there are computer programs to
show the construction step by step, also where
possible, co-ordinates have been used to indicate
particular hole positions. These read from the bottom
left-hand corner of the component side, with the
horizontal co-ordinate given first.

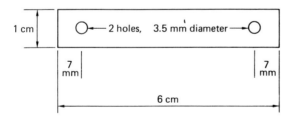

Figure 2.3   Cable clamp

To simplify assembly, we now include a step-by-step
computer program. This program graphically shows the
component side of the circuit board; it shows where the
board is drilled and where each of the 20 wires are
soldered to it. The program is not essential, but
should help assembly.

```
 10 REM Listing 2.1-Link board assy
 20 MODE2
 30 VDU23;8202;0;0;0;
 40 VDU23,241,0,0,40,16,16,16,40,0
 50 A$=" wire from left "
 60 *FX11,0
 70 PROCgrid
 80 PROCstep1
 90 PROCstep2
100 PROCstep3
110 PROCstep4
120 PROCstep5
130 END
140 :
150 DEFPROCgrid
160 VDU28,18,31,18,14
170 COLOUR 2:PRINT"COMPONENT SIDE"
180 COLOUR 7:VDU28,18,10,18,0
190 FOR X=0 TO 1056 STEP 32
200 FOR Y=40 TO 640 STEP 24
210 IF X*Y MOD5=0 THEN GCOL0,2 ELSE GCOL0,7
220 PLOT 69,X,Y:NEXT Y,X:A=GET:ENDPROC
230 :
240 DEFPROCstep1
250 COLOUR 1:PRINT"STEP 1"
260 VDU5:GCOL0,1
270 FOR N=1 TO 6
280 READ X,Y:MOVE X,Y:PRINT"*":NEXT N
290 DATA 36,100,228,100,772,100,964,100
300 DATA 36,604,964,604
310 VDU4,30:A=GET:ENDPROC
320 :
330 DEFPROCstep2
340 COLOUR 2:PRINT"STEP 2"
350 VDU5:GCOL0,2
360 FOR X=328 TO 680 STEP 32
370 MOVE X,200:PRINTCHR$(241)
380 NEXT X:VDU4,30:A=GET:ENDPROC
390 :
400 DEFPROCstep3
410 COLOUR 3:PRINT"STEP 3":GCOL0,3
420 MOVE 336,640:DRAW 720,640
430 DRAW 720,568:DRAW336,568
440 DRAW 336,640
450 VDU30:A=GET:ENDPROC
460 :
470 DEFPROCstep4
480 PRINT"STEP 4"
490 MOVE 224,40:DRAW 832,40
500 DRAW 832,136:DRAW 224,136
510 DRAW 224,40:GCOL0,7
520 MOVE 396,0:DRAW 396,36
530 PLOT 85,708,36:MOVE 708,0
540 PLOT 85,396,0
550 VDU30:A=GET:ENDPROC
560 :
570 DEFPROCstep5
580 COLOUR 6:PRINT"STEP 5"
```

```
590 GCOL0,6:VDU26
600 FOR N=0 TO 7
610 MOVE 468+N*32,140
620 DRAW 388,208+N*48
630 PRINTTAB(0,8);N*2+5;"th"A$
640 A=GET:NEXT N
650 GCOL0,1:COLOUR 1
660 MOVE 396,140:DRAW 356,208
670 PRINTTAB(0,8);"1st"A$
680 A=GET:MOVE 436,140:DRAW 356,256
690 PRINTTAB(0,8);"3rd"A$
700 A=GET:GCOL0,5:COLOUR 5
710 FOR N=0 TO 9
720 MOVE420+N*32,140:DRAW 420+N*32,540
730 IF N=0 THEN PRINTTAB(0,8)"2nd"A$
740 IF N>0 THEN PRINTTAB(0,8);N*2+2;"th"A$
750 A=GET:NEXT N:ENDPROC
```

When the program has been typed in and run, it will
stop at each stage until a key is pressed. Before
getting too enthusiastic with a soldering iron, it is
worth doing a ´dry run´ to ensure that all the
instructions are clear. That is, go through each step
without actually doing any cutting or soldering.

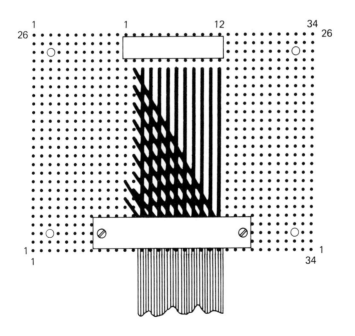

Figure 2.4 Link board layout, component side

Step 1
Drill 4 mounting holes [(3,3), (32,3), (3,24), (32,24)] and the two holes for the cable clamp [(9,3), (26,3)] with a 3.5 mm drill in the positions shown. The Veroboard needs to be drilled carefully, otherwise it tends to crack; it is best drilled from the track side.

Step 2
Cut the 12 copper tracks shown [(12,7), (13,7), (14,7), etc. up to (23,7)] using the 3.5 mm drill or a Veroboard cutter. It is necessary only to drill through the copper track, not right through the board. It is quite easy to drill the copper track with a hand-held drill bit provided that it is sharp! Cutting these tracks prevents the cable clamp from shorting out the tracks to the socket.

Step 3
Solder the 12-way Minicon socket on to the component side of the board. Make sure that the socket faces the edge of the board. Take care not to bridge the gaps between the tracks of the Veroboard with solder.

Step 4
Lay the cable on the component side of the board so that the end of the cable just goes over the socket. Place one of the cable clamps under the board and one on top of the cable and bolt the two together. Do not screw the clamps so tight that the board bends, but make sure that it is tight enough to stop the cable being pulled out.

Step 5
This is the tedious part. First separate the 20 wires from the end back to the cable clamp. Take one wire at a time, cut it a little longer than needed and strip just under 1 cm of the insulation off, taking care not to damage the copper conductor. One mistake will mean starting all over again! Then tin the wire, feed it into the correct hole on the board, and solder it in place. Again check that no solder bridges are formed. The conductor positions are numbered from left to right of the cable looking at the component side, with the cable clamp at the bottom of the board.

Conductor	Position	Conductor	Position
1	(12, 8)	11	(13,14)
2	(14,22)	12	(19,22)
3	(12,10)	13	(13,16)
4	(15,22)	14	(20,22)
5	(13, 8)	15	(13,18)
6	(16,22)	16	(21,22)
7	(13,10)	17	(13,20)
8	(17,22)	18	(22,22)
9	(13,12)	19	(13,22)
10	(18,22)	20	(23,22)

At this stage it is worth while leaving the completed board, and then later checking it carefully for mistakes.

There are alternative methods of connecting the cable to the board. These are easier to do, but are more expensive. It is possible to buy another IDC connector and mating circuit board socket (as fitted to the BBC microcomputer), and to solder the circuit board socket to the board. As the pins solder to adjacent holes on the Veroboard, it is necessary to cut the copper tracks between two adjacent holes, not the usual method of cutting the track at a hole. This can be done only with a sharp knife and a steady hand. The other method is to use an IDC circuit board connector, which is clamped on to the cable and solders directly on to the circuit board. These connectors are not easy to obtain however.

Now all the User Port connections have been brought out to the 12-way Minicon socket. Numbering the socket from left to right with the IDC cable to the bottom and looking at the component side of the board, they appear as follows

Pin 1	5 volt line
Pin 2	0 volt line
Pin 3	CB1
Pin 4	CB2
Pin 5	PB0
Pin 6	PB1
Pin 7	PB2
Pin 8	PB3
Pin 9	PB4
Pin 10	PB5
Pin 11	PB6
Pin 12	PB7

THE SWITCH BOARD
The simplest form of input into the User Port is a switch. This is used to switch the input line low (it normally floats high). To switch all the inputs it is necessary to have a bank of eight switches. This is where cost rears its ugly head again. Circuit board mounting switches are not easy to get hold of and eight such switches can prove to be quite expensive. A cheap alternative is to use an 8-way, dual-in-line (DIL) switch. These have the advantage that they are cheap and make wiring into the circuit simple, but they have the disadvantage that they are rather small to operate.

Components Required

```
1 piece 0.1 Veroboard, 34 tracks by 26 holes
1          8-way single throw DIL switch
1          12-way 0.1 pitch Minicon plug
           (right-angled)
           Tinned copper link wire
```

Construction
Cut the Veroboard to size and smooth the edges. The assembly details are included in the following computer program.

```
  10 REM Listing 2.2-Switch board assy
  20 MODE2
  30 VDU23;8202;0;0;0;
  40 VDU23,241,0,0,40,16,16,16,40,0
  50 *FX11,0
  60 PROCgrid
  70 PROCstep1
  80 PROCstep2
  90 PROCstep3
 100 PROCstep4
 110 END
 120 :
 130 DEFPROCgrid
 140 VDU28,18,31,18,12
 150 COLOUR 2:PRINT"COMPONENT SIDE"
 160 VDU28,18,10,18,0
 170 FOR X=0 TO 1056 STEP 32
 180 FOR Y=40 TO 640  STEP 24
 190 IF X*Y MOD5=0 THEN GCOL0,2 ELSE GCOL0,7
 200 PLOT 69,X,Y:NEXT Y,X:A=GET:ENDPROC
 210 :
 220 DEFPROCstep1
 230 COLOUR 3:PRINT"STEP 1"
 240 GCOL0,3:FOR N=0 TO 11
 250 MOVE 352+N*32,0:DRAW 352+N*32,64
```

```
260 NEXT N:GCOL0,4:FOR N=0 TO 3
270 MOVE 352,40+4*N:DRAW 704,40+4*N
280 NEXT N:VDU30:A=GET:ENDPROC
290 :
300 DEFPROCstep2
310 COLOUR 2:PRINT"STEP 2"
320 VDU5:GCOL0,2:FOR N=0 TO 7
330 MOVE 456+32*N,316:PRINTCHR$241:NEXT N
340 VDU4,30:A=GET:ENDPROC
350 :
360 DEFPROCstep3
370 COLOUR 3:GCOL0,3:PRINT"STEP 3"
380 MOVE 464,264:DRAW 720,264
390 DRAW 720,368:DRAW 464,368
400 DRAW 464,264
410 VDU30:A=GET:ENDPROC
420 :
430 DEFPROCstep4
440 COLOUR 5:PRINT"STEP 4"
450 GCOL0,5:FOR N=0 TO 3
460 MOVE 480+N*64,424:DRAW 512+N*64,424
470 NEXT N:FOR N=0 TO 2
480 MOVE 512+N*64,472:DRAW 544+N*64,472
490 NEXT N:MOVE 480,472:DRAW 384,472
500 ENDPROC
```

Once the program has been typed in, go through each
stage doing a 'dry run' to check that you understand
the instructions. Also see figures 2.5 and 2.6.

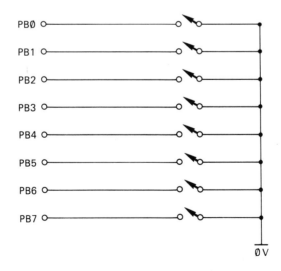

Figure 2.5 Switch board circuit diagram

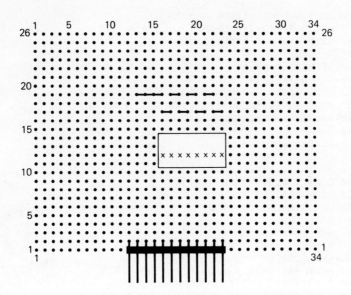

Figure 2.6   Switch board layout, component side

Step 1
Fit the 12-way Minicon plug on to the board and solder
each pin. Take care not to bridge the tracks with
solder.

Step 2
Using a spot-face cutter or a hand-held 3.5 mm drill
bit cut the 8 tracks shown. [(16,12), (17,12), (18,12),
(19,12), (20,12), (21,12), (22,12), (23,12)]. These are
the right-hand 8 tracks of the circuit board that the
multicon plug has been soldered to. Remember that the
co-ordinates and the diagrams are all referenced to the
component side of the board.

Step 3
Fit the DIL switch in position and solder it in place.
It should fit so that the cut tracks are all under the
switch.

Step 4
Use tinned copper wire to wire in the 8 links shown.
They do not need to be insulated with sleeving. These
links connect one side of each of the switches to the 0
volt line.

                link (16,17) to (17,17)
                link (18,17) to (19,17)
                link (20,17) to (21,17)

```
link (22,17) to (23,17)
link (13,19) to (16,19)
link (17,19) to (18,19)
link (19,19) to (20,19)
link (21,19) to (22,19)
```

This board is now complete and the link board can now be tested. Before connecting anything up, switch off the computer, connect the link board to the User Port, and plug the switch board into the link board. Ensure that the boards are always connected so that the component side is always uppermost. Now switch the computer on and if it does not power up correctly, switch off again immediately and check all the connections again. Now type in the following program to test the boards.

```
10 REM listing 2.3-User Port Input
20 CLS
30 ?&FE62=0 :REM Program PB0-PB7 as inputs
40 REPEAT
50 N=?&FE60 :REM Read port B
60 PRINTTAB(0,12)"Number at User Port is ";N;"   "
70 I=INKEY(50)
80 UNTIL 0
```

?&FE62=0 sets all 8 bits of the User Port to input. Lines 40 to 80 form an infinite REPEAT...UNTIL loop. Line 50 peeks into location &FE60 to read the value at the User Port. If all the switches are off it will read 0, if they are all on it will read 255. Line 70 is a half-second delay.

To look at any particular line, where the value of the other lines is not known, the logical operator AND can be used. For example, to check on the status of PB3 we could say

```
IF (?&FE60 AND 8) = 8 THEN ...
```

or to wait for PB1 to go to logic 0 we could say

```
REPEAT
UNTIL (?&FE60 AND 2) = 0
```

THE LED BOARD

This board contains 8 LEDs (Light-Emitting Diodes), one for each bit of the User Port. The outputs from the 6522 VIA can just supply enough current to drive one LED directly, but it is better to provide some form of buffer circuit to drive the LED. This could be a transistor circuit or an IC. As an IC has a lower component count and is cheaper to buy than the discrete components, a circuit has been designed around an IC. A TTL (transistor-transistor logic) chip is used to switch the LED on and off in this circuit. The current required to switch the TTL load is well within the safe working range of the 6522. Several chips could have been used for this purpose, but one of the commonest and easiest to use is the 7400. This is a TTL quad NAND gate (figure 2.7). Its internal circuit is shown in figure 2.6. A 7400 chip with an LS designation (74LS00) could equally well be used for this application. The LS indicates that the chip is a low-power variety. Two 7400 chips are required to drive all 8 LEDs.

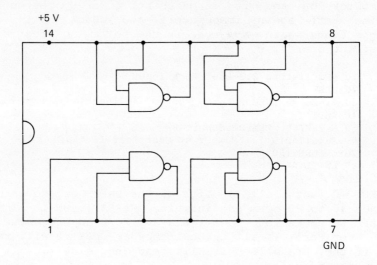

Figure 2.7   The 7400 quad NAND gate viewed from above

Only one of the two inputs of each NAND gate needs to be used, the other is ´tied´ to the +5 volt line through a 1 Kohm resistor. A 220 ohm resistor is placed in series with each LED to limit the current to a safe level. Figure 2.8 shows the circuit, and figure 2.9 the board layout.

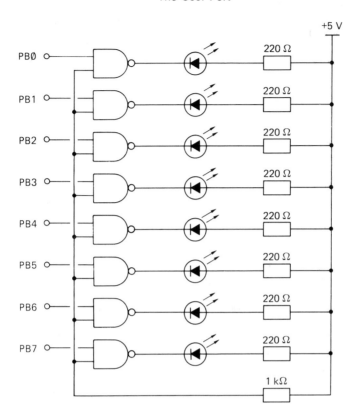

Figure 2.8   Circuit diagram of LED board

Components Required

```
1 piece 0.1 Veroboard, 34 tracks by 40 holes
1 12-way  Minicon socket (right-angled)
1         12-way Minicon plug
1         1 Kohm resistor
8         220 ohm resistor
2         14 pin IC sockets
2         74LS00 IC
8         Red LED
2         0.1 µF disc ceramic capacitor
          Tinned copper wire
          Coloured sleeving
```

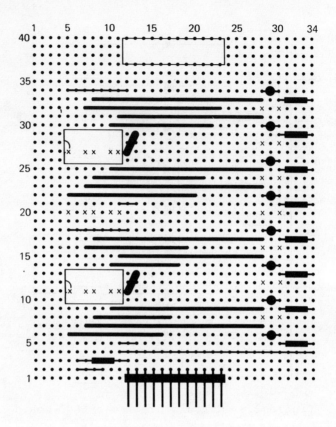

Figure 2.9   LED board layout, component side

Construction

This board looks complicated but is quite easy to assemble if it is taken stage by stage. The following program shows each stage graphically.

```
 10 REM Listing 2.4-LED board assy
 20 MODE2
 30 VDU23,241,0,0,40,16,16,16,40,0
 40 VDU23,242,16,56,124,124,124,124,56,16
 50 VDU23;8202;0;0;0;
 60 *FX11,0
 70 PROCgrid
 80 PROCstep1
 90 PROCstep2
100 PROCstep3
110 PROCstep4
120 PROCstep5
130 PROCstep6
```

```
140 PROCstep7
150 PROCstep8
160 PROCstep9
170 END
180 :
190 DEFPROCgrid
200 VDU28,18,31,18,12
210 COLOUR 2:PRINT"COMPONENT SIDE"
220 COLOUR 7:VDU28,18,10,18,0
230 FOR X=0 TO 1056 STEP 32
240 FOR Y=40 TO 976 STEP 24
250 IF X*Y MOD5=0 THEN GCOL0,2 ELSE GCOL0,7
260 PLOT 69,X,Y:NEXT Y,X:A=GET:ENDPROC
270 :
280 DEFPROCstep1
290 COLOUR 3:PRINT"STEP 1"
300 GCOL0,3:FOR N=0 TO 11
310 MOVE 352+N*32,0:DRAW 352+N*32,64
320 NEXT N:GCOL0,4:FOR N=0 TO 3
330 MOVE 352,40+4*N:DRAW 704,40+4*N
340 NEXT N:VDU30:A=GET:ENDPROC
350 :
360 DEFPROCstep2
370 PRINT"STEP 2":GCOL0,3:MOVE 336,904
380 DRAW 720,904:DRAW 720,976
390 DRAW 336,976:DRAW 336,904
400 VDU30:A=GET:ENDPROC
410 :
420 DEFPROCstep3
430 COLOUR 2:PRINT"STEP 3"
440 VDU5:GCOL0,2:FOR N=1 TO 29
450 READ X,Y:MOVE X*32-56,Y*24+32:PRINTCHR$241:NEXT N
460 DATA 5,11,7,11,8,11,10,11,11,11
470 DATA 5,20,7,20,8,20,10,20,11,20
480 DATA 5,27,7,27,8,27,10,27,11,27
490 DATA 28,8,28,12,28,16,28,20
500 DATA 28,24,28,28,28,32
510 DATA 30,8,30,12,30,16,30,20
520 DATA 30,24,30,28,30,32
530 VDU4,28,18,10,18,0,30:A=GET:ENDPROC
540 :
550 DEFPROCstep4
560 COLOUR 3:PRINT"STEP 4":GCOL0,3
570 FOR N=0 TO 384 STEP 384
580 MOVE 112,244+N:DRAW 336,244+N
590 DRAW 336,340+N:DRAW 112,340+N
600 DRAW 112,244+N:MOVE 120,276+N
610 DRAW 120,312+N:MOVE 128,288+N
620 DRAW 128,300+N:NEXT N
630 A=GET:VDU30:ENDPROC
640 :
650 DEFPROCstep5
660 COLOUR 3:PRINT"STEP 5"
670 GCOL0,3:FOR N=0 TO 7
680 MOVE 928,136+N*96:DRAW 1056,136+N*96
690 FOR T=0 TO 20 STEP 4
700 MOVE 960,128+N*96+T:DRAW 1024,128+N*96+T
710 NEXT T,N:MOVE 160,88:DRAW 352,88
```

```
 720 FOR N=0 TO 20 STEP 4
 730 MOVE 224,76+N:DRAW 288,76+N:NEXT
 740 FOR N=0 TO 384 STEP 384:FOR T=0 TO 16 STEP 8
 750 MOVE 344+T,280+N
 760 DRAW 376+T,328+N:NEXT T,N
 770 VDU4,28,18,10,18,0,30:A=GET:ENDPROC
 780 :
 790 DEFPROCstep6
 800 COLOUR 1:PRINT"STEP 6"
 810 VDU5:GCOL0,1:FOR N=0 TO 7
 820 MOVE 864,160+N*96:DRAW 928,160+N*96
 830 MOVE 872,176+N*96:PRINTCHR$242:NEXT
 840 VDU4,28,18,10,18,0,30:A=GET:ENDPROC
 850 :
 860 DEFPROCstep7
 870 COLOUR 4:PRINT"STEP 7":GCOL0,4
 880 FOR N=1 TO 6:READ x,X,Y
 890 MOVE x,Y:DRAW X,Y:NEXT N
 900 DATA 160,256,64,352,1056,112
 910 DATA 320,384,136,128,352,448
 920 DATA 320,384,520,128,352,832
 930 A=GET:VDU30:ENDPROC
 940 :
 950 DEFPROCstep8
 960 COLOUR 5:PRINT"STEP 8":GCOL0,5
 970 FOR N=1 TO 4:READ X,Y
 980 FOR T=0 TO 384 STEP 384
 990 MOVE X,Y+T:DRAW 864,Y+T:NEXT T,N
1000 DATA 192,184,288,232,320,376,224,424
1010 A=GET:VDU30:ENDPROC
1020 :
1030 DEFPROCstep9
1040 COLOUR 6:PRINT"STEP 9":GCOL0,6
1050 FOR N=0 TO 3:READ X,Y
1060 FOR T=0 TO 1
1070 MOVE X,Y+T*384:DRAW 480+(N+T*4)*32,Y+T*384
1080 NEXT T,N
1090 DATA 120,160,224,208,288,352,192,400
1100 ENDPROC
```

Step 1

First check that the board has been cut to the correct size. The tracks should run the longest way. Solder the 12-way Minicon plug on to the Veroboard in the position shown.

Step 2

Solder the 12-way Minicon socket on to the Veroboard.

Step 3

There are 29 breaks to be made in the tracks. Use a spot-face cutter, or a hand-held 3.5 mm drill bit. Remember, the screen display shows the component side of the board, and not the track side. If in doubt, mark each hole to be cut with a felt-tipped pen and check

before the tracks are cut. The breaks are at the
following co-ordinates

(5,11), (7,11), (8,11), (10,11), (11,11)
(5,20), (7,20), (8,20), (10,20), (11,20)
(5,27), (7,27), (8,27), (10,27), (11,27)
(28,8), (28,12), (28,16), (28,20), (28,24), (28,28),
(28,32)
(30,8), (30,12), (30,16), (30,20), (30,24), (30,28),
(30,32)

Step 4
Fit the two 14-pin integrated circuit sockets and
solder them in position. Ensure that if there is a
notch on the socket it is placed the correct way round.
Sometimes pin 1 is marked, in that case pin 1 is
located in the bottom left-hand corner as the board is
displayed on the screen. Do not fit the ICs at this
stage. A difficulty that can occur is that the socket
does not sit properly on the board. This is one time
when one needs three hands, one for the soldering iron,
one for the solder and one to hold the socket to the
board. An easy way to get the sockets flush on to the
board using only two hands is to solder only the two
opposite corner pins. Then, squeezing the socket firmly
against the board, re-apply the soldering iron to the
two joints until the socket is flush with the board,
then solder the rest of the pins.

Step 5
Solder the eight 220 ohm resistors, the 1 Kohm resistor
and the two 0.1 μF disc ceramic capacitors in place.
The eight 220 ohm resistors fit down the right-hand
edge of the board, the 1 Kohm resistor fits next to the
Minicon plug, and the two capacitors are fitted
diagonally across the +5 volt and the 0 volt lines next
to the IC sockets. These have to be fitted diagonally
as the two power lines are on adjacent tracks. When
fitting the resistors, it is good practice always to
put the colour bands so that they read correctly when
the board is viewed from the bottom.

Step 6
Next fit the eight LEDs. The LEDs must be fitted the
correct way round or they will not work. The anode has
the longer lead and should be placed to the right, next
to the 220 ohm resistor.

Step 7
Fit the six links shown. Two links connect the 0 volt
line to pin 7 of the ICs. Two links connect the 5 volt

line to pin 14 of the ICs. One link takes 5 volts to the eight LED current-limiting resistors. The last link links pin 2 to pin 5 (and also pin 10 to pin 13) of the ICs. These links do not need sleeving.

Step 8
Now fit the eight links from pins 3, 6, 8 and 11 of each IC to the respective LEDs. These links will need sleeving because of their close proximity to other links.

Step 9
Fit the eight links from pins 1, 4, 9 and 12 of both ICs to the 8 lines from the User Port. (Plug connections 5 to 12.)

Step 10
Check that the board has been assembled correctly and if necessary run through the computer program again. Check for bridges of solder across the tracks, and to ensure that tracks have been cut correctly. At this stage do not insert the two ICs, but connect the board to the link board and plug the link board into the computer. Each LED can be tested by linking pin 7 of the IC sockets to the respective pins in turn: pins 3, 6, 8 and 11. Use a small length of tinned copper wire to test each LED. The most likely fault if some do not work is that they have been wired the wrong way round.

Once all the LEDs work, switch off and insert the two ICs into their sockets. Ensure that the notch is to the left, or the dot is in the bottom left-hand corner.

Now the board can be tested fully. Type in the following short program

```
10 REM listing 2.5-LED board test
20 ?&FE62=&FF :REM program PB0-PB7 as outputs
30 REPEAT
40 ?&FE60=255 :REM write to port B
50 I=INKEY(100)
60 ?&FE60=0    :REM write to port B
70 I=INKEY(100)
80 UNTIL 0
```

This program should switch on the bank of eight LEDs at one go and switch them off again. Line 20 sets all eight bits of the User Port to output. Line 40 switches all the outputs on, line 60 switches them all off again. Lines 50 and 70 give a 1-second delay. The following three programs (listings 2.6 to 2.9) switch the lights on and off again in different sequences.

```
10 REM listing 2.6-Light sequencer 1
20 ON ERROR RUN
30 CLS
40 PRINT´CHR$141"           LIGHT SEQUENCER 1"
50 PRINTCHR$141"           LIGHT SEQUENCER 1"´´´
60 INPUT"Time delay in centiseconds "T
70 ?&FE62=&FF :REM program PB0-PB7 as outputs
80 REPEAT
90 FOR N=0 TO 7
100 ?&FE60=2^N :REM write to port B
110 I=INKEY(T)
120 NEXT N
130 UNTIL 0
```

```
10 REM listing 2.7-Light sequencer 2
20 ON ERROR RUN
30 CLS
40 PRINT´CHR$141"           LIGHT SEQUENCER 2"
50 PRINTCHR$141"           LIGHT SEQUENCER 2"´´´
60 INPUT"Time delay in centiseconds "T
70 ?&FE62=&FF :REM program PB0-PB7 as outputs
80 REPEAT
90 FOR N=0 TO 7
100 ?&FE60=2^N :REM write to port B
110 I=INKEY(T)
120 NEXT N
130 FOR N=6 TO 1 STEP-1
140 ?&FE60=2^N :REM write to port B
150 I=INKEY(T)
160 NEXT N
170 UNTIL 0
```

```
10 REM listing 2.8-Light sequencer 3
20 ON ERROR RUN
30 CLS
40 PRINTTAB(11,2)CHR$141"LIGHT SEQUENCER 3"
50 PRINTTAB(11,3)CHR$141"LIGHT SEQUENCER 3"
60 INPUTTAB(3,6)"Time delay in centiseconds "T
70 ?&FE62=&FF :REM program PB0-PB7 as outputs
80 FOR N=0 TO 255
90 ?&FE60=N :REM write to port B
100 PRINTTAB(16,12)CHR$131 CHR$141;N
110 PRINTTAB(16,13)CHR$131 CHR$141;N
120 I=INKEY(T)
130 NEXT N
```

Listing 2.9 allows the user to display in binary any number between 0 and 255. The number is entered through the keyboard.

```
10 REM listing 2.9-Binary number display
20 ?&FE62=&FF :REM program PB0-PB7 as outputs
30 REPEAT
40 INPUT"Enter a number between 0 and 255 "num
50 ?&FE60=num :REM write to port B
60 UNTIL 0
```

This program does not check that the number entered is within the range 0 to 255. What is the effect of entering numbers outside that range?

Lastly enter in listing 2.3 again. Now with the LED board still connected to the link board, connect the switch board to the LED board socket. Each LED will now indicate whether the appropriate switch is on or off. Hence the LED board can be used not only as an output state indicator, but also as an input state indicator.

3 Using the User Port

By now the reader should have some appreciation of how the User Port operates, and some understanding of how the 8 lines can be programmed as outputs or inputs. This chapter will look at some of the range of devices that can be connected to the User Port. The system of boards introduced in chapter 2 will be extended and developed to allow an even greater flexibility of application. Many of the ideas in this chapter should be taken as a starting point for one's own ideas, and not be seen as the ultimate possibilities for the User Port.

With the User Port set to output, there are three types of device that it should be able to handle. First, it should be able to operate a low-power device such as an LED or a piezo-electric buzzer. Second, it should be able to drive a high-power device such as a relay or an electric motor; third, it should be able to make use of a range of specialist integrated circuits to perform special functions. From these three types of device, a wide range of control applications becomes available to the user.

To set the User Port to input, essentially the only functions required are a switching function and an ability to interface with other specialist digital integrated circuits, such as an analogue-to-digital converter. The switching function can be performed in a variety of ways. It can be a simple toggle switch, a push-to-make switch, a light-activated switch, etc.

A BUFFER BOARD

In chapter 2 the boards were driven directly from the 6522 VIA. This simple option works well in practice provided that only one TTL load is being driven from the User Port. However, for some applications it is useful to be able to drive several TTL loads at once. The 6522 VIA will provide a current of only 1.6 mA, sufficient to drive one standard TTL load. It cannot therefore drive more than one circuit without some external help. The answer is to put a buffer between the User Port and these loads. There are difficulties.

For instance, each line of the User Port can be
configured as either output or input, independent of
the rest. To provide a buffer board offering such
facilities would need 16 buffers (8 for input, 8 for
output) together with 8 switches to switch each line
from output to input. A simpler and cheaper alternative
that is suitable for many applications is to be able to
switch four lines at a time. That can be achieved using
one of several TTL tri-state buffers or transceivers.
These come in quad or octal form. A tri-state buffer
has a misleading name - it is not a digital logic with
three logic levels, it is just ordinary logic with a
third output state: open circuit. A separate enable
input is used to put the output into the third state,
regardless of the logic levels present at the buffer's
input.

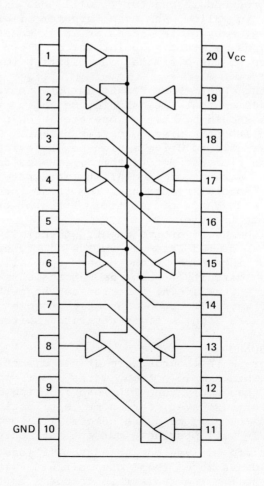

Figure 3.1   The 74LS244 tri-state buffer

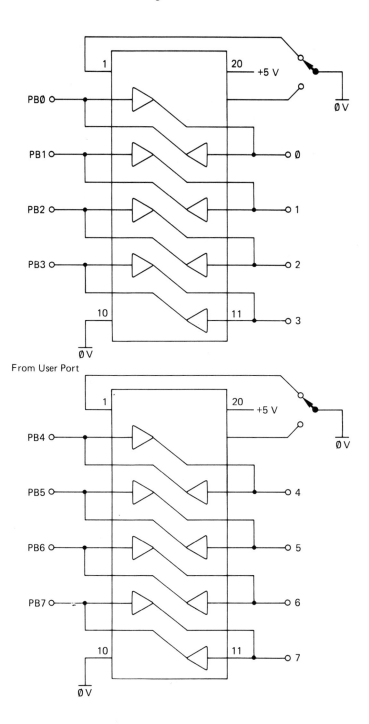

Figure 3.2   Circuit diagram of the buffer board

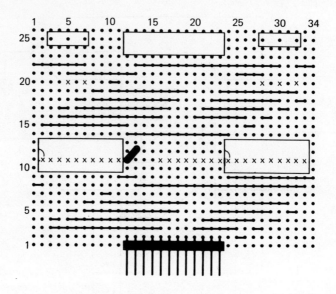

Figure 3.3   Buffer board layout

Integrated circuits 74LS240 to 74LS245 provide a range of tri-state buffers, both inverting and non-inverting, to suit most purposes, and will source a current of 24 mA, suitable for driving up to 15 standard TTL loads or 60 low power TTL loads. The device chosen for this application was the 74LS244 quad transceiver, tri-state. This is a chip with two sets of four buffers each with its own enable line. Two of these chips are needed for the buffer board, to provide the sixteen buffers needed. They are readily available and cheap, and it is worth buying a spare in case of accidents! They are 20-pin devices, and purchasing 20-pin sockets is not all that easy, but it is essential in this application so that the buffer can be replaced if needed. The switches could prove to be an awkward component to obtain. If circuit board mounting switches cannot be obtained then miniature dual-in-line switches are a possibility, otherwise miniature switches with solder tag connections could be fastened to the board with standoffs and connected with wire links to the board. See figures 3.1, 3.2 and 3.3.

Components required

1 piece	0.1 Veroboard, 34 tracks by 26 holes
1	12-way 0.1 pitch Minicon plug (right-angled)
1	12-way 0.1 pitch Minicon socket (right-angled)
2	20-pin IC sockets
2	74LS244 octal buffers
2	Single-pole changeover switch (circuit board mounting)
1	0.1 μF disc ceramic capacitor
	Tinned copper wire

Construction

The board contains many links but is otherwise uncomplicated to build. Some variation from this layout might be needed if similar switches cannot be obtained.

```
 10 REM Listing 3.1 Buffer board assy
 20 MODE 1
 30 MODE2
 40 VDU23;8202;0;0;0;
 50 VDU23,241,0,0,40,16,16,16,40,0
 60 *FX11,0
 70 PROCgrid
 80 PROCstep1
 90 PROCstep2
100 PROCstep3
110 PROCstep4
120 PROCstep5
130 PROCstep6
140 END
150 :
160 DEFPROCgrid
170 VDU28,18,31,18,12
180 COLOUR 2:PRINT"COMPONENT SIDE"
190 VDU28,18,10,18,0
200 FOR X=0 TO 1056 STEP 32
210 FOR Y=40 TO 640 STEP 24
220 IF X*Y MOD5=0 THEN GCOL0,2 ELSE GCOL0,7
230 PLOT 69,X,Y:NEXT Y,X:ENDPROC
240 :
250 DEFPROCstep1
260 COLOUR 3:PRINT"STEP 1"
270 GCOL0,3:FOR N=0 TO 11
280 MOVE 352+N*32,0:DRAW 352+N*32,64
290 NEXT N:GCOL0,4:FOR N=0 TO 3
300 MOVE 352,40+4*N:DRAW 704,40+4*N
310 NEXT N
320 GCOL0,3:MOVE 336,568
330 DRAW 720,568:DRAW 720,640
340 DRAW 336,640:DRAW 336,568
350 VDU30:A=GET:ENDPROC
360 :
370 DEFPROCstep2
```

```
380 GCOL0,2:COLOUR 2:PRINT"STEP 2"
390 VDU5:FOR N=0 TO 31
400 IF N>9 AND N<14 THEN GOTO420
410 MOVE N*32+8,296:VDU241
420 NEXT N
430 FOR N=1 TO 5:READ X
440 MOVE X*32+8,512:VDU241
450 NEXT N
460 DATA 3,5,26,28,30
470 VDU4,30:A=GET:ENDPROC
480 :
490 DEFPROCstep3
500 GCOL0,3:COLOUR 3:PRINT"STEP `3"
510 FOR X=16 TO 720 STEP 704
520 MOVE X,244:DRAW X+320,244
530 DRAW X+320,340:DRAW X,340
540 DRAW X,244
550 MOVE X+8,276:DRAW X+8,308
560 MOVE X+16,284:DRAW X+16,300
570 NEXT X:FOR T=0 TO 16 STEP 8
580 MOVE 344+T,256:DRAW 376+T,312
590 NEXT T:VDU30:A=GET:ENDPROC
600 :
610 DEFPROCstep4
620 COLOUR 1:PRINT"STEP 4"
630 FOR X=48 TO 848 STEP 800:GCOL0,1
640 MOVE X,592:MOVE X+160,592
650 PLOT 85,X+160,640
660 MOVE X,640:PLOT85,X,592
670 FOR N=0 TO 2:GCOL0,7
680 PLOT 69,X+16+N*64,616
690 PLOT 69,X+16+N*64,620
700 NEXT N,X:VDU30:A=GET:ENDPROC
710 :
720 DEFPROCstep5
730 GCOL0,6:COLOUR 6:PRINT"STEP 5"
740 FOR N=1 TO 11
750 READ X1,X2,Y
760 MOVE X1*32,Y*24+40:DRAW X2*32,Y*24+40
770 NEXT N
780 DATA 0,1,7, 10,12,8, 12,32,7
790 DATA 23,33,8, 1,11,14, 11,23,13
800 DATA 4,12,20, 24,27,20, 0,6,21
810 DATA 12,29,21, 31,33,21
820 VDU30:A=GET:ENDPROC
830 :
840 DEFPROCstep6
850 GCOL0,5:COLOUR 5:PRINT"STEP 6"
860 FOR N=1 TO 16
870 READ X1,X2,Y
880 FOR T=0 TO 1
890 MOVE (T+X1)*32,T*312+Y*24+40
900 IF T=1 AND X2-X1=1 THEN X2=X2+1
910 DRAW X2*32,T*312+Y*24+40
920 NEXT T,N
930 DATA 2,15,2, 4,16,3, 6,17,4
940 DATA 8,18,5, 2,3,3, 4,5,4
950 DATA 6,7,5, 8,9,6, 24,19,2
```

```
960 DATA 26,20,3, 28,21,4, 30,22,5
970 DATA 24,25,1, 26,27,2, 28,29,3
980 DATA 30,31,4
990 VDU30:A=GET:ENDPROC
```

Step 1
Solder the 12-way Minicon plug and socket on to the component side of the Veroboard.

Step 2
Cut the tracks where shown on the diagram. There are 33 breaks to be made in the track, although this number will vary slightly if different switches are used. Remember that the diagram refers to the component side, yet the cuts need to be made on the track side.

Step 3
Solder the two 20-pin IC sockets in place. Solder the disc capacitor across the 5 volt and 0 volt lines adjacent to the IC socket. Do not fit the ICs at this stage. If there is a pin 1 marking or a notch on the sockets, it should be to the left.

Step 4
Fit the two circuit board mounting switches. Ensure that they do not extend beyond the top of the board, otherwise it will not be possible to connect up other boards.

Step 5
Fit the eleven links as shown in cyan on the screen display. These links connect +5 volts to pin 10 of each IC, and 0 volts to pin 20. Also pins 1 and 19 of each IC, the enable pins, are linked to the switches. The switch wiper is connected to 0 volts. Notice that there is no link for pin 19 of the left-hand IC; the track connects the switch directly.

Step 6
Wire in the links shown in magenta on the screen display for each line of the User Port. There are sixteen links connecting the plug to the ICs and sixteen links connecting the socket to the ICs.

Step 7
Once the board has been completed and checked, fit the two ICs. Pin 1 is the bottom left-hand pin of each IC, as the board is displayed.

AN INPUT/OUTPUT DISPLAY PROGRAM
When developing extra boards to add to the system it is

useful to have one program that will quickly and easily allow the User Port to act as either input or output. Listing 3.2 is a program that will display a number at the User Port both as a number and also in the form of a bit pattern. Although this program is by no means the most compact program that will display such information, it does have several graphics routines that improve the screen display. There is a double-height routine and a routine to draw large letters on the screen. Both of these routines work by calling the OSWORD routine at &FFF1. The OSWORD routine invokes a number of miscellaneous operations all of which require more parameters, or all of which produce more results than can be passed in A, X and Y. OSWORD calls are usually used in assembly language, but they can be called from BASIC programs if the integer variables A%, X% and Y% are set. If A% is set to 10 (&A), this OSWORD call reads a character definition. The dot pattern for each character displayed on the screen is stored in eight bytes. This call enables the eight bytes to be read into a block of memory starting at an address given in X% and Y%. In this program the X% and Y% point to locations &D00 onwards. The double-height routine simply takes the dot pattern and prints each dot twice vertically. The large-letter routine prints each dot out as a full character. Thus the numbers are printed out eight times as big. By defining a character that is a rectangular block slightly smaller than full character size, an attractive number display is formed. It is more readable than if the full character size had been printed. This character has the ASCII code 254 and is defined in line 160. A new character definition could be put here if so desired.

```
 10 REM Listing 3.2 Input/Output display
 20 ON ERROR RUN
 30 REPEAT
 40 MODE1
 50 PROCinitialise
 60 PROCboxes
 70 PROCdouble("DIGITAL CONTROL",12,2)
 80 PRINTTAB(0,6)"Select INPUT (I) or OUTPUT (O) ";
 90 A$=GET$
100 PRINTTAB(0,6) SPC(32)
110 IF A$="I" THEN PROCdouble("INPUT ",16,5)
    :PROCinput
120 IF A$="O" THEN PROCdouble("OUTPUT",16,5)
    :PROCoutput
130 UNTIL 0
140 :
150 DEFPROCinitialise
```

```
160 VDU23,254,0,126,126,126,126,126,126,0
170 VDU23,255,255,255,255,255,255,255,255,255
180 VDU23;8202;0;0;0;
190 VDU19,0,4,0,0,0
200 VDU19,3,6,0,0,0
210 X%=0:Y%=&D:A%=10:D=&D00
220 B$=CHR$255+CHR$8+CHR$10+CHR$255+CHR$11
230 B$=B$+B$+B$
240 C$=CHR$(240)+CHR$8+CHR$10+CHR$(241)
250 ENDPROC
260 :
270 DEFPROCboxes
280 COLOUR 2
290 PRINTTAB(7,9)STRING$(26,CHR$255)
300 FOR Y=10 TO 18
310 PRINTTAB(7,Y)CHR$255 SPC(24) CHR$255
320 NEXT Y
330 PRINTTAB(7,19)STRING$(26,CHR$255)
340 a$=CHR$255+"    "
350 PRINTTAB(3,21)STRING$(33,CHR$255)
360 PRINTTAB(3,22)STRING$(8,a$)CHR$255
370 PRINTTAB(3,23)STRING$(8,a$)CHR$255
380 PRINTTAB(3,24)STRING$(33,CHR$255)
390 PRINTTAB(4,26)"128  64  32  16  8   4   2   1"
400 COLOUR 3
410 ENDPROC
420 :
430 DEFPROCoutput
440 ?&FE62=&FF
450 REPEAT
460 PRINTTAB(2,30)
    "Enter a number between 0 and 255     "
470 COLOUR 1:INPUTTAB(35,30)J
480 IF J<0 OR J>255 GOTO470
490 COLOUR 3:PROCbiglet(J)
500 PROCblock(J)
510 ?&FE60=J
520 UNTIL 0
530 ENDPROC
540 :
550 DEFPROCinput
560 ?&FE62=0
570 check=0
580 REPEAT
590 REPEAT
600 J=?&FE60
610 UNTIL J<>check
620 PROCbiglet(J)
630 PROCblock(J)
640 check=J
650 UNTIL0
660 ENDPROC
670 :
680 DEFPROCdouble(A$,x,y)
690 FOR N=1 TO LEN(A$)
700 ?D=ASC(MID$(A$,N,1)):CALL&FFF1
710 VDU23,240,D?1,D?1,D?2,D?2,D?3,D?3,D?4,D?4
720 VDU23,241,D?5,D?5,D?6,D?6,D?7,D?7,D?8,D?8
```

```
730 PRINT TAB(x+N-1,y)C$
740 NEXT N
750 ENDPROC
760 :
770 DEFPROCbiglet(num)
780 A$=STR$(J)
790 IF LEN(A$)<3 A$=" "+A$:GOTO790
800 FOR N=1 TO 3
810 ?D=ASC(MID$(A$,N,1)):CALL&FFF1
820 FOR row=1 TO 8:PRINTTAB(8*N,10+row);
830 FOR line=1 TO 8
840 IF (D?row AND 2^(8-line))>0 THEN VDU254 ELSE
VDU32
850 NEXT line,row,N
860 ENDPROC
870 :
880 DEFPROCblock(num)
890 COLOUR 1
900 FOR N=0 TO 7
910 IF (num AND 2^N)=0 THEN COLOUR 0:ELSE COLOUR 1
920 PRINTTAB(32-4*N,22)B$
930 NEXT N
940 COLOUR 3
950 ENDPROC
```

AN OUTPUT MOTHER BOARD

When building interfacing applications for the User
Port, it is a great deal easier if there is a series of
ready-made building bricks or black boxes that can be
plugged together to make a system. Most of the
requirements are quite simple. A traffic light
demonstration requires three different coloured LEDs. A
pelican crossing requires an extra two LEDs and, if one
wants to do it properly, a buzzer. Both demonstrations
could be each built on to purpose-designed boards that
would plug into the link board, or directly into the
User Port.

Although more complicated at first, it is better to
build a mother board into which daughter boards
containing such simple devices can be plugged (see
figures 3.4 and 3.5). Then traffic light demonstrations
or pelican crossing demonstrations can be built and the
parts re-used for further demonstrations. This cuts
down cost in the long run and greatly simplifies new
applications. If desired, it is still possible to build
purpose-made systems once the prototype system has been
proved.

Rather than having one board to handle all eight
outputs, two boards each handling four outputs are
outlined here. They are very similar in construction.
(If required, one large board could of course be
constructed.) These utilise the 40 hole size board, and
a new component, the vertical pin Minicon plug. Four

6-pin Minicon plugs are fixed to each board, and the
output devices are built on very small daughter boards
which plug into the mother board. The plugs and sockets
are polarised to prevent the boards from being
incorrectly fitted. It sounds complicated, but once
built the versatility of the system will be
appreciated.

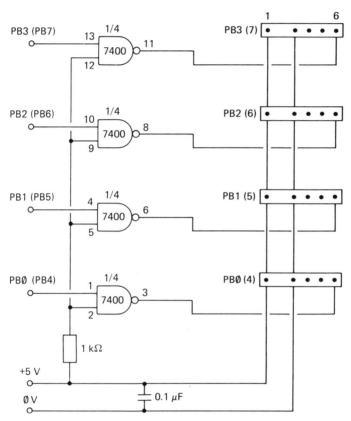

Figure 3.4   Circuit diagram of the output mother board

Components Required (for each board)

1 piece	0.1 Veroboard, 34 tracks by 40 holes
1	12-way 0.1 pitch Minicon plug (right-angled)
1	12-way 0.1 pitch Minicon socket (right-angled)
4	6-way 0.1 pitch Minicon plug (vertical)
1	14-pin IC socket
1	7400 IC (note not the low power variety)
1	0.1 μF disc ceramic capacitor
1	1 Kohm resistor
	Tinned copper wire

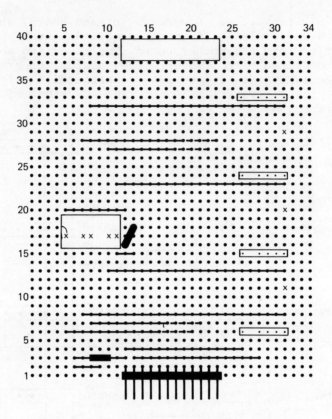

Figure 3.5   Output mother board layout

Construction

The construction of the mother board should present no
problems, it is similar in design to the LED board. If
it is wished to output all eight bits of the User Port,
two such boards will be required. The boards are almost
identical, except that the positions of four of the
signal links are different. This is indicated on the
screen and in figure 3.5 by the dotted links.

```
 10 REM Listing 3.3 Output mother board assembly
 20 MODE2
 30 VDU23,241,0,0,40,16,16,16,40,0
 40 VDU23,242,16,56,124,124,124,124,56,16
 50 VDU23;8202;0;0;0;
 60 *FX11,0
 70 PROCgrid
 80 PROCstep1
 90 PROCstep2
100 PROCstep3
```

```
110 PROCstep4
120 PROCstep5
130 PROCstep6
140 END
150 :
160 DEFPROCgrid
170 VDU28,18,31,18,12
180 COLOUR 2:PRINT"COMPONENT SIDE"
190 COLOUR 7:VDU28,18,10,18,0
200 FOR X=0 TO 1056 STEP 32 .
210 FOR Y=40 TO 976 STEP 24
220 IF X*Y MOD5=0 THEN GCOL0,2 ELSE GCOL0,7
230 PLOT 69,X,Y:NEXT Y,X:A=GET:ENDPROC
240 :
250 DEFPROCstepl
260 COLOUR 3:PRINT"STEP 1"
270 GCOL0,3:FOR N=0 TO 11
280 MOVE 352+N*32,0:DRAW 352+N*32,64
290 NEXT N:GCOL0,4:FOR N=0 TO 3
300 MOVE 352,40+4*N:DRAW 704,40+4*N
310 NEXT N:GCOL0,3:MOVE 336,904
320 DRAW 720,904:DRAW 720,976
330 DRAW 336,976:DRAW 336,904
340 FOR N=0 TO 648 STEP 216
350 MOVE 784,148+N:DRAW 976,148+N
360 DRAW 976,172+N:DRAW 784,172+N
370 DRAW 784,148+N:NEXT N
380 VDU30:A=GET:ENDPROC
390 :
400 DEFPROCstep2
410 COLOUR 2:PRINT"STEP 2"
420 VDU5:GCOL0,2:FOR N=1 TO 8
430 READ X,Y:MOVE X*32-24,Y*24+32:PRINTCHR$241:NEXT N
440 DATA 4,17,6,17,7,17,9,17,10,17
450 DATA 30,11,30,20,30,29
460 VDU4,28,18,10,18,0,30:A=GET:ENDPROC
470 :
480 DEFPROCstep3
490 COLOUR 3:PRINT"STEP 3":GCOL0,3
500 MOVE 112,388:DRAW 336,388
510 DRAW 336,484:DRAW 112,484
520 DRAW 112,388:MOVE 120,420
530 DRAW 120,456:MOVE 128,432
540 DRAW 128,444
550 A=GET:VDU30:ENDPROC
560 :
570 DEFPROCstep4
580 COLOUR 7:PRINT"STEP 4":GCOL0,7
590 MOVE 160,88:DRAW 352,88
600 FOR N=0 TO 20 STEP 4
610 MOVE 224,76+N:DRAW 288,76+N:NEXT
620 FOR T=0 TO 16 STEP 8
630 MOVE 344+T,400
640 DRAW 376+T,448:NEXT T
650 VDU4,28,18,10,18,0,30:A=GET:ENDPROC
660 :
670 DEFPROCstep5
680 COLOUR 5:PRINT"STEP 5":GCOL0,5
```

```
690 FOR N=1 TO 5:READ X1,X2,Y
700 MOVE X1*32,Y*24+40:DRAW X2*32,Y*24+40:NEXT N
710 DATA 5,8,1, 12,27,2, 11,25,3
720 DATA 10,12,14, 4,11,19
730 A=GET:VDU30:ENDPROC
740 :
750 DEFPROCstep6
760 COLOUR 6:PRINT"STEP 6":GCOL0,6
770 FOR N=1 TO 8:READ X1,X2,Y
780 MOVE X1*32,Y*24+40:DRAW X2*32,Y*24+40:NEXT N
790 FOR N=1 TO 4:READ X1,X2,Y
800 MOVE X1*32,Y*24+40:PLOT21,X2*32,Y*24+40:NEXT N
810 DATA 4,15,5, 7,16,6, 6,30,7
820 DATA 9,30,12, 10,30,22, 9,17,26,
830 DATA 6,18,27, 7,30,31, 15,19,5,
840 DATA 16,20,6, 17,21,26, 18,22,27
850 ENDPROC
```

Step 1
Fit the 12-way Minicon plug, and the 12-way Minicon
socket. Next take the four 6-way vertical Minicon plugs
and remove pin 2 from each of them. If locating pins
are fitted to the appropriate sockets, then this will
prevent the boards from being inserted incorrectly, or
the input boards from being plugged in by mistake. Then
fit the four plugs into the circuit board and, ensuring
that the plugs are vertical, solder them in place.

Step 2
Cut the tracks in the 8 positions shown in figure 3.5
or shown on the screen.

Step 3
Fit the integrated circuit socket. Do not fit the
integrated circuit until the board is complete.

Step 4
Fit the 1 Kohm resistor from the 5 volt line to pin 2
of the IC and the disc ceramic capacitor between the 5
volt and 0 volt tracks next to the IC socket.

Step 5
Fit the 5 links shown which supply 5 volts and 0 volts
to the IC and the 4 plugs. One link connects pin 2 to
pin 5 of the IC (and pins 10 and 13).

Step 6
Fit the 8 signal links. This is where the difference
between the two boards comes in, one board outputs bits
0 to 3, shown by the solid links, and the second board
outputs bits 4 to 7, shown by the solid links including
the dotted sections.

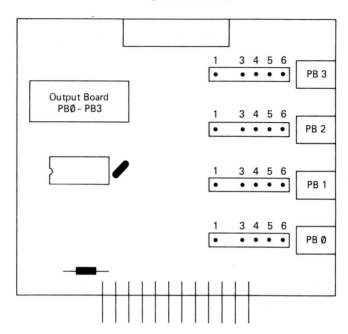

Figure 3.6   Output mother board PB0-PB3

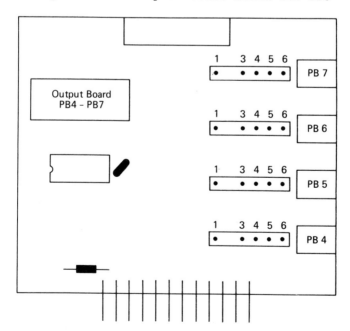

Figure 3.7   Output mother board PB4-PB7

Step 7

Once the board is assembled, fit the 7400 IC. It is not advisable to use the low-power versions (74LS00, 74S00 or 74H00) for this purpose as they cannot provide sufficient output current to drive some of the applications listed later in the chapter. A standard 7400 NAND gate will source 16 mA, whereas the 74LS00 will source only 4 mA.

Next it is necessary to label the board and each plug, otherwise it is all too easy to use the wrong board and wonder why the circuit does not work with the controlling software. Figures 3.6 and 3.7 show how each board should be labelled. Labelling can be done by writing on the Veroboard using a fine-point indelible felt-tipped pen, or by using self-adhesive labels cut to size.

Output Modules

Once the two output mother boards have been built then a variety of output daughter modules can be plugged into any of the eight plugs. The daughter boards are made from small pieces of Veroboard 12 tracks wide and 24 holes long. A right-angled 6-way Minicon socket is soldered at the bottom to plug into the mother board. A polarising key is fitted at position 2 of the socket. Figure 3.8 shows the dimensions of the boards.

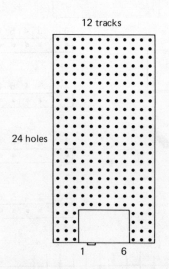

Figure 3.8   Daughter board dimensions

The connections to the socket are shown below.

Socket	Connection
1	+5 volts
2	Polarising key
3	0 volts
4	No connection
5	No connection
6	Buffered output

A LED module

The LED module is very easy to construct. It consists of a daughter board with a 6-pin socket plus the LED and a 220 ohm resistor. Figure 3.9 shows the circuit diagram and the layout of the circuit board. The NAND gate is also shown on the circuit diagram although this is part of the mother board. The components on the LED module are shown in the dotted box.

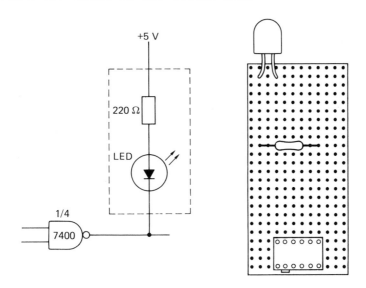

Figure 3.9   LED circuit diagram and board layout

The construction of the board involves fitting the socket and the two components. As the daughter boards are fitted vertically, it is necessary to bend the LED over so that it points up above the end of the board. It should be noted that the value of the resistor can be reduced to increase the brightness of the LED. A green LED requires a greater current to achieve the same brightness as a similar red LED, and the resistor value needs to be dropped to 180 or 150 ohms to compensate. A polarising key should be fitted to the socket at position 2 (from the left, component side) to prevent the board from being incorrectly fitted.

A buzzer module

Piezo-electric buzzers are small buzzers with an amazingly loud output. They are the sort of buzzers that are used in digital watches fitted with alarms, and in some calculators. They have a very small size and they will work from a supply as low as 3.5 volts. This makes them suitable for use in the output board circuit. The circuit and board layout are shown in figure 3.10. The variable resistor or potentiometer is not essential, but is worth including as these buzzers are very piercing and it is better to be able to reduce the volume if necessary. It is a small multi-turn potentiometer, as these can be adjusted from above, and has pin spacings that are the same pitch as the Veroboard.

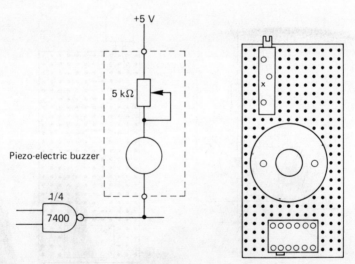

Figure 3.10   Buzzer circuit diagram and board layout

A relay module

The relay module can be used to switch a variety of devices that require a voltage above 5 volts, or that require a higher current than the NAND gate can safely supply. Examples here are electric motors and high-power relays. The basic relay module described here uses a reed switch relay. Reed relays have the advantages of low cost and low power consumption so that they can be driven directly by NAND gates without any extra circuitry. (There are many types of relay

available, some with changeover switching, and some
which are double pole. Provided that they are rated at
5 volts and have a coil resistance greater than 250
ohms then they can be used in a similar way.) Figure
3.11 shows the circuit diagram and the layout of the
circuit board. The layout shown is for a single reed
relay with ´open coil´. Some reed relays come in the
same package sizes as integrated circuits. They are
generally more expensive than the ´open coil´ type used
here. The diode is of the type 1N914 or 1N4008. It is
fitted to the board because the inductive effect of the
relay coil can damage the NAND gate. (A diode must
always be placed across the coil for circuit protection
with any relay, although some of the reed relays in
14-pin DIL packages already have the diode fitted
internally.) The cathode of the diode (the end
connected to +5 volts) is usually marked on the diode
by a coloured band near the end. If fitted the wrong
way round, current will flow down the diode rather than
through the relay coil and the circuit will not work.

The relay switch connections are brought out from
the board by using a printed circuit terminal block.
These small screw terminal blocks solder on to the
Veroboard and allow wires to be connected without
soldering. There is one track to be cut on this board,
that is between the two coil pins of the relay.

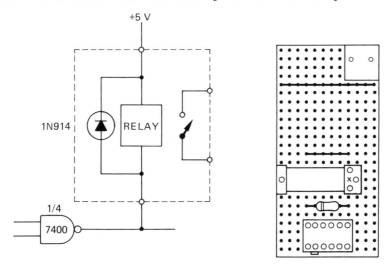

Figure 3.11 Relay circuit diagram and board layout

AN OPTO-ISOLATOR MODULE
An opto-isolator performs roughly the same task as a
relay, although it is less robust. As its name

suggests, it is used to isolate an output from an
input. It provides a high degree of protection between
the output board (and hence the computer) and any
device connected to its output. Therefore it can be
used in the same way as the relay to isolate against
high-voltage applications. Opto-isolators will not
handle as high a current or voltage as a relay but they
have the advantage of speed and there are no moving
parts to go wrong. They each come packaged as a 6-pin
integrated circuit. Figure 3.12 shows the internal
circuit of two common opto-isolators and figure 3.13
the layout. The pin connections for both are the same.
The maximum continuous power rating for the output side
of the device is 150 milliwatts.

Under the opto-isolator, the Veroboard tracks must
be cut.

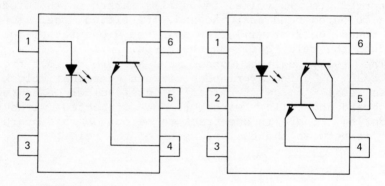

Figure 3.12 Opto-isolators, internal circuits

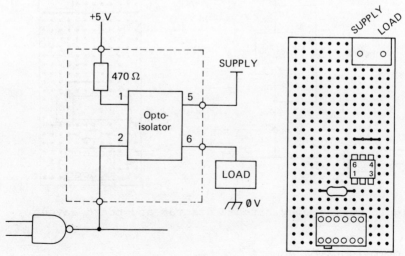

Figure 3.13 Opto-isolator circuit diagram
and board layout

AN INPUT MOTHER BOARD

This board (figures 3.14 and 3.15) is split into two, each inputting four lines to the User Port, in the same way in which the output mother boards are arranged. Essentially, these boards are the same as the output boards, except for the connections to the IC, and a different pin on each plug is used to polarise the plug. One useful feature of such plugs is that free sockets can be purchased with wire connectors so that switches of various sorts can easily be connected to the system with flying leads.

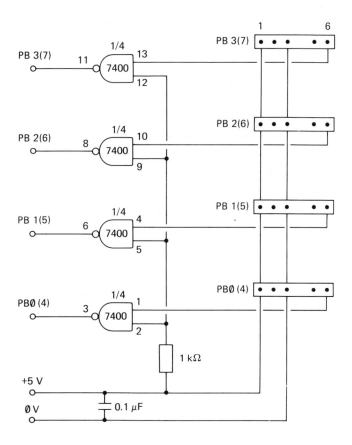

Figure 3.14   Circuit diagram of the input mother board

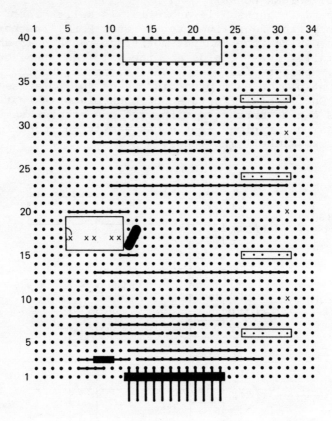

Figure 3.15   Input mother board layout

Components Required (for each board)

1 piece	0.1 Veroboard, 34 tracks by 40 holes
1	12-way 0.1 pitch Minicon plug (right-angled)
1	12-way 0.1 pitch Minicon socket (right-angled)
4	6-way 0.1 pitch Minicon plug (vertical)
1	14-pin IC socket
1	7400 IC (note, not the low-power variety)
1	0.1 μF disc ceramic capacitor
1	1 Kohm resistor
	Tinned copper wire

Construction

The construction of the boards is the same as the output board. Listing 3.3 can be used but needs to have three lines changed.

```
810 DATA 6,15,5, 9,16,6, 4,30,7
820 DATA 7,30,12, 9,30,22, 10,17,26
830 DATA 7,18,27, 6,30,31, 15,19,5
```

These changes reflect the different link connections to the IC.

Construction of the board is identical except that the locating pin is changed to pin 4 (see step 1). Again it is necessary to label the boards. With four very similar boards, it is all too easy to get the wrong one.

A SEVEN-SEGMENT DISPLAY

As well as connecting up a range of devices such as LEDs, switches and relays, this board system can be used to interface with a whole series of specialist TTL or CMOS integrated circuits. To demonstrate this, a seven-segment display can be connected to the User Port. This display needs to have a combination of the bars illuminated to represent each of the numbers from 0 to 9. It would be possible to get a computer program to do the work of presenting the correct combination of outputs to represent the numbers. The display could simply be connected to the User Port in the same manner as described for the LED display of chapter 2. However the purpose here is not to go back to ´nut and bolt´ level but to see how easy interfacing can be in practice. There exists an integrated circuit, the 7447, which is a BCD to seven-segment display decoder/driver. In other words it requires a 4-bit binary input, and will convert the output to suit a seven-segment display output. The output current is sufficient to drive a display without any extra buffering being required. The pin connections can be seen in figure 3.16.

Pin 3 is a lamp test, which when held low will light all the segments of the display at once. There are several other inputs which make the chip more versatile but these are not required for this application. When RBI (ripple blanking input) is low and the four data inputs, DCBA, are low, all outputs are high (off) and RBO (Ripple Blanking Output) goes low. When BI is held low, all outputs are off regardless of the level of any other input. Thus, unwanted leading 0s in a multi-segment display can be blanked.

PIN CONNECTION

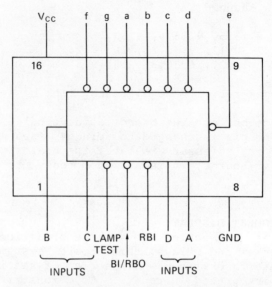

Figure 3.16   7447 BCD to 7-segment decoder/driver

The binary input can handle numbers in the range
0-15; however, the display can only display numbers in
the range 0-9. The chip is programmed to display
numbers above 9 as a unique pattern that verifies
operation of the chip (see figure 3.17).

Figure 3.17   7447 BCD to 7-segment decoder/driver
              Numerical designations and resultant displays

The seven-segment display used is a general-purpose
0.5 inch common-cathode display. The connection diagram
for it is shown in figure 3.18. There are a variety of
such displays, and provided that they are of the
common-cathode variety, they are quite easy to connect
to the 7447. The display also has an integral decimal
point.

Figure 3.18   7-segment display

Pin	Function
1	Segment e
2	Segment d
3	Common cathode
4	Segment c
5	Decimal point
6	Segment b
7	Segment a
8	Common cathode
9	Segment f
10	Segment g

The circuit is very simple. A resistor is required in the line from the IC to each segment to reduce the current. A 330 ohm resistor is recommended to give a good illumination. There needs to be a 0.1 μF capacitor across the 7447 supply lines, and the input connections are as follows

                    PB0 to pin 7
                    PB1 to pin 1
                    PB2 to pin 2
                    PB3 to pin 6

The construction of the board (figure 3.19) is similar to several of the boards described earlier. It is necessary to connect only one common-cathode, although on the layout shown both are connected. The board can be tested using the program given at the start of this chapter. Using this program, all the sixteen outputs can be observed. The patterns formed by the 13 and 14 inputs can be utilised to provide an ´E´ to indicate overflow.

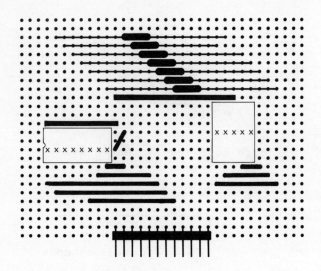

Figure 3.19   7-segment display board layout

```
 10 REM Listing 3.4
 20 REM 7-segment display
 30 ?&FE62=&FF
 40 ?&FE60=15
 50 REPEAT
 60 INPUT"Enter a number "num
 70 IF num<0 OR num>9 PROCerror ELSE PROCoutput(num)
 80 UNTIL 0
 90 :
100 DEFPROCerror
110 VDU7
120 TIME=0
130 REPEAT
140 ?&FE60=13
150 ?&FE60=14
160 UNTIL TIME>500
170 ?&FE60=15
180 ENDPROC
190 :
200 DEFPROCoutput(N)
210 ?&FE60=N
220 ENDPROC
```

Listing 3.4 is a routine to display a digit in the
range 0 to 9, and outside that range the display will
show a letter ´E´. Line 30 switches all the data lines
to output, although strictly speaking only the first
four need switching to output. Line 40 outputs the
number 15. This blanks the display. The program then
asks for a number to be input, and checks the range. If

it is within the required range, the display will show
the same number; if outside the required range, the
computer will bleep and a letter ´E´ will be displayed.
Notice that because of the way the ´E´ is formed, the
top bar appears fainter than the rest. As the computer
is able to switch the display off and on extremely
quickly, no flashing is evident. Line 170 is included
to blank the display after 5 seconds.

HANDSHAKING LINES CB1 AND CB2

As well as the eight data lines PB0-PB7 the User Port
has two handshaking lines, CB1 and CB2. These too can
be programmed as either input lines or output lines. In
the input mode they represent one standard TTL load,
and in the output mode they will drive one standard TTL
load. (The data lines PB0-PB7 will output sufficient
current, 1 mA, to drive a Darlington transistor
circuit; CB1 and CB2 will not.) In practice, the
handshaking lines are required in applications only
where the BBC microcomputer is being connected to
another computer or piece of equipment that is as
complicated as the computer itself. The Printer Port
uses similar lines because the printer works at a
different speed from the computer, and cannot handle
information as fast as the computer is able to send it.
Therefore to avoid loss of data, the printer signals
through a control line when it is ready to receive
information. The computer also signals to the printer
when it has information to transmit. The information
itself is transmitted along eight data lines.

The handshaking lines are controlled by the PCR
(Peripheral Control Register), at memory location
&FE6C. This register controls not only CB1 and CB2 but
also CA1 and CA2 (these are used by the Printer Port)
and the 8 bits control the handshaking lines, as shown
in figure 3.20.

PCR0	CA1 control
PCR1	CA2 control bit 1
PCR2	CA2 control bit 2
PCR3	CA2 control bit 3
PCR4	CB1 control
PCR5	CB2 control bit 1
PCR6	CB2 control bit 2
PCR7	CB2 control bit 3

Figure 3.20 The peripheral control register

The CA1 and CB1 lines can each set bits in another
VIA register, the Interrupt Flag Register, IFR. The
memory location of this register is &FE6D. The CB1

control bit governs when the bits are set in the IFR. If the control bit is set to 0 then bit 4 in the Interrupt Flag Register will be set when the voltage goes from high to low. A change from high to low is called a negative edge or a falling edge. If the control bit is set to 1, then bit 4 in the Interrupt Flag Register is set when the voltage on the input line goes from low to high. A change from low to high is called a positive or rising edge. Notice that this is different from the data lines in that the condition which sets the bit is not the voltage level itself but the change in voltage levels. Such inputs are known as edge-triggered inputs. The CB2 (and CA2) control bits have the following effects.

PCR 7	PCR 6	PCR 5	Effect
0	0	0	Input mode. CB1 interrupt flag set on negative edge of signal. Flag cleared by read/write of ORB/IRB
0	0	1	Input mode. CB1 interrupt flag set on negative edge of signal. Flag cleared by writing to IFR
0	1	0	Input mode. CB1 interrupt flag set on positive edge of signal. Flag cleared by read/write of ORB/IRB
0	1	1	Input mode. CB1 interrupt flag set on positive edge of signal. Flag cleared by writing to IFR
1	0	0	Output mode. CB2 set high by an active transition of CB1. Reset by read/write of ORB/IRB
1	0	1	Output mode. CB2 goes low for one cycle following a read/write of ORB/IRB
1	1	0	Output mode. CB2 always low
1	1	1	Output mode. CB2 always high

The CB2 flag is bit 3 of the interrupt flag register. The most useful of these eight modes of operation of CB2 for simple interfacing projects are the last two, where CB2 is set either high or low.

4 The Analogue Port

The Analogue Port is to be found at the rear of the BBC microcomputer. It is a 15-pin ´D type´ connector. The Analogue Port has four analogue-to-digital converters, two switch inputs, and a light-pen input. The connections are shown in figure 4.1.

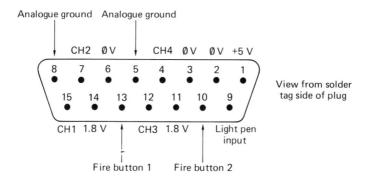

Figure 4.1   The Analogue Port

The switch inputs are actually connected to the 6522 VIA chip (VIA A) which handles all the keyboard inputs, and outputs to the sound and speech processors. (There are two 6522 VIA chips in the BBC, the other, VIA B, handles the User and Printer Ports.) The Analogue Port also has two digital inputs. These are included for use with joysticks when they are used for the fire buttons.

The four analogue-to-digital inputs provided are 12-bit integrating converters. The four channels can be selected under software control. By applying a voltage beween 0 volts and 1.8 volts to any of the channel inputs, a number in the range 0 to 65520 will be generated which is directly proportional to the voltage in. The number 65520 might seem a rather strange one to have as a maximum. Usually the computer has convenient round numbers (in hexadecimal notation). The reason here is that when the computer was designed, the best analogue-to-digital converters available would work only to a resolution of 12 bits (2^{12} which equals 4096, or gives a range of 0 to 4095). It was hoped that devices would become available which would allow up to 16 bit resolution (2^{16} which equals 65536, or has a range of 0 to 65535). Hence each number at present is multiplied by 16, or increases in steps of 16. Therefore the highest number is 4095 x 16 which equals 65520.

Reading a value at any of the channels is done using the ADVAL statement. To put the value read by the channel 1 analogue-to-digital converter into the variable X, the following syntax is used

        X=ADVAL(1)

Similarly for the other three channels

        X=ADVAL(2)
        X=ADVAL(3)
        X=ADVAL(4)

The ADVAL statement also has other uses. ADVAL(0) can be used to test the fire buttons, and also to check which was the last analogue-to-digital channel to complete conversion.

        X=ADVAL(0) AND 3

will give a number with the following meaning

        X=0 ... No fire button pressed
        X=1 ... Left fire button pressed
        X=2 ... Right fire button pressed
        X=3 ... both fire buttons pressed

        X=ADVAL(0) DIV 256

will give the number of the last analogue-to-digital channel to complete conversion. If the value returned is zero then no channel has yet completed conversion.

ADVAL with a negative number in the brackets can be used to test the state of the various internal buffers in the computer. The User Guide should be consulted for further details about these.

The analogue-to-digital chip used in the BBC computer is the μPD7002. It will sense an analogue input in the range 0 volts to 1.8 volts. A voltage above 1.8 volts could be considered harmful. In fact this chip will stand any voltage that does not exceed the supply voltage of the chip, although the manufacturers warn that sustained voltages near the supply voltage will reduce the life of the chip. As the supply voltage is 5 volts, any voltage equal to or below 5 volts should be safe for the analogue-to-digital converter. The best supply to use is that provided by the computer itself at pin 1. As this voltage is the same as that supplied to the chip itself, there is little chance of blowing the chip. If the reader uses an external supply, then great care must be taken never to exceed 5 volts. For most applications the current drawn from the 5 volt supply provided through the Analogue Port is minimal, so that it is better to use this supply. All the applications covered in this chapter use the 5 volt supply from the Analogue Port, and the current used is well within the capabilities of the BBC microcomputer´s power supply.

It can be seen from figure 4.1 that there is a convenient 1.8 reference voltage at pins 11 and 14 of the Analogue Port. The reader might assume that this is the best supply to use for the sensors. In practice it is far better to use a 5 volt supply and reduce it down to 1.8 volts by a resistor network, as the 1.8 volt reference is not a very stable source. It is derived from the 5 volt supply by three diodes, each of which can be expected to drop 0.6 volts. In use, this reference voltage is unreliable. It depends on the current being drawn across the diodes, and it also drifts with temperature. That is to say, as the diodes warm up the voltage drop across them changes. For the rest of this chapter, and in the applications given in chapters 6 and 7, the 5 volt supply is used with a resistor included in the line to drop the voltage if necessary. It is possible to buy devices that will give a very stable reference voltage. These should be considered where an accurate reading is essential.

On the Analogue Port connector there is a 0 volt connection at pin 2, and two analogue ground connections at pins 5 and 8. The latter two are electrically the same and should be used as the ground for the analogue inputs, rather than the 0 volt line.

*FX CALLS FOR THE ANALOGUE PORT
As well as the BASIC ´ADVAL´ statement there are several *FX calls that can be used to program the analogue-to-digital input. Each analogue-to-digital conversion takes 10 milliseconds to complete; that gives 40 milliseconds for all four channels. If time is important, it is possible to select only some of the channels for conversion using *FX16.

*FX16,0   Disable all analogue-to-digital
           sampling

```
*FX16,1    Sample channel 1
*FX16,2    Sample channels 1 and 2
*FX16,3    Sample channels 1, 2 and 3
*FX16,4    Sample all four channels
```

Once a channel has been disabled, an ADVAL call to that channel will return the last conversion figure before the channel was disabled.

For some applications it is useful to be able to have an up-to-date sample. As has been seen above, it is possible for a sample to be up to 40 milliseconds old. This might not seem long, but it is a long time in computing terms. *FX17 can be used to force a conversion on a particular channel. It will work even if that channel has previously been disabled using *FX16.

```
*FX17,1    Force an analogue-to-digital
           conversion on channel 1
*FX17,2    Force an analogue-to-digital
           conversion on channel 2
*FX17,3    Force an analogue-to-digital
           conversion on channel 3
*FX17,4    Force an analogue-to-digital
           conversion on channel 4
```

EXPLORING THE ANALOGUE PORT

In chapter 3, a mother/daughter board system was described for the User Port. The advantages of such a system are that it simplifies the construction of new projects, it cuts down the cost of the special User Port plug and cable, and it saves time in the long run. Similarly, the Analogue Port has an expensive plug, and to build several projects for the Analogue Port, each with its own plug, can prove rather costly. Therefore a similar mother board has been designed for the Analogue Port (see figures 4.2 and 4.3). It enables devices to be easily constructed and then plugged into the mother board in a foolproof manner using a far cheaper interconnection system. Later it is easy to use such devices in projects simply and safely.

The mother board uses the same type of connector as does the User Port mother board, and has a similar construction. A quick look at the board layout will show the main differences that will be experienced between the User Port and the Analogue Port. There are many fewer links, and no buffer circuits are needed. The mother board is the same size as the User Port

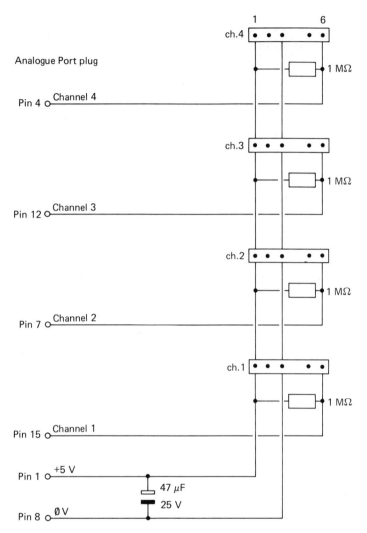

Figure 4.2   Circuit diagram of the mother board

mother board, mainly for convenience. The input sockets
are wired in the same way as the input sockets for the
User Port, and some of the sensing devices used on the
User Port can also be used for the Analogue Port and
vice versa. The reader should be aware that some
devices are essentially digital devices and   some
analogue devices; so if, say, an analogue device is
used on a digital input, it will not function in the
same way as it would with the Analogue Port.

     The electrolytic capacitor is fitted across the +5
volt line and the analogue ground line to minimise
spurious voltage fluctuations.   The four 1 Mohm
resistors are placed in the circuit to pull each

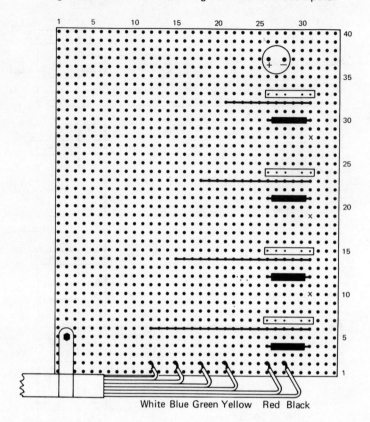

White Blue Green Yellow   Red Black

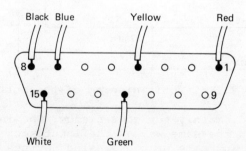

Figure 4.3   Layout of the mother board

analogue channel up to just above 2 volts. The value of
these resistors is so high that they will cause little
interference to any component inserted in the circuit,
but they do ensure that a channel with no sensor
connected will not give a random reading but will
always read the maximum (65520). At this point the
reader is probably wondering why the resistor is not
placed between ground and the analogue input, thereby

pulling the input to 0. The reason is that to pull the
analogue input down to 0, the resistor value would need
to be much smaller in value; it would then interfere
with some sensors and affect the input voltage. These
resistors are not essential, but when the mother board
is used with the test program given later, the
resistors prevent fluctuating readings from being
displayed.

Components required

1 piece	0.1 pitch Veroboard, 34 tracks by 40 holes	
4	6-way 0.1 pitch Minicon plugs (vertical)	
4	1 Mohm resistor	
1	47 μF 6.4 V electrolytic capacitor circuit board mounting	
1	15-pin ´D type´ plug	
1	15-pin ´D type´ plug cover	
1 metre	6-core cable	
1	´P´ clip 3/16 inch	
1	3 mm nut and bolt	
6	Veropins	
	Tinned copper wire	

Construction
The Analogue Port mother board is not difficult to
construct, and so no step-by-step program is needed.
Apart from the links and integrated circuit, the board
is similar in layout to the User Port input mother
board.

Step 1
Push the six Veropins into the board [(12,2), (15,2),
(18,2), (21,2), (26,2) and (28,2)] and solder. These
are small pins that are a push fit into the board, and
are used to form posts on to which wires can be
connected.

Step 2
Cut the tracks in the three places shown [(31,10),
(31,19) and (31,28)]. Drill a 3.5 mm hole in the
position shown [(2,5)]. Remember that these co-
ordinates are given from the component side, and that
the tracks are to be cut on the track side.

Step 3
Remove pin 4 from each of the four 6-way Minicon plugs,
fit in the positions shown and solder. Removing pin 4
allows the plugs to be polarised, as was done with the
User Port boards.

Step 4
Solder the four links in position. These link the
Veropins to pin 6 of each of the input plugs.

Step 5
Solder the four 1 Mohm resistors in the positions
shown. Solder the electrolytic capacitor in position.
Take care to ensure that the polarity is correct. Note
that the voltage rating of the capacitor can be greater
if a 6.4 volt rating is difficult to obtain.

Step 6
Strip 8 cm of the outer cover of the 6-way cable. Clamp
the cable to the board using the ´P´ clip and the 3 mm
nut and bolt in the position shown. Then cut each wire
2 cm beyond its Veropin, strip and tin the end and
solder in place.

Step 7
Strip 4 cm of the other end of thc outer cover of the
cable, and strip and tin 0.5 cm of each wire. Solder
the wires to the ´D type´ plug and fit the cover. Do
ensure that the cable clamp is secure. At this point
check that the plug will fit properly into the Analogue
Port. With early BBC microcomputers, or with some types
of plug covers, the opening in the computer case is not
large enough, and it must be enlarged using a sharp
knife. (Always direct the cutting blade away from the
fingers!)

The mother board connections
The four plugs on the mother board are wired in the
same way, except that each plug serves a different
analogue channel.

Pin 1	+5 volts
Pin 2	No connection
Pin 3	Analogue ground
Pin 4	Polarising pin
Pin 5	No connection
Pin 6	Analogue input

AN ANALOGUE PORT TEST PROGRAM
This program is included to simplify the testing and
investigation of devices to be connected to the
Analogue Port. It shows the status of each of the four
channels of the Analogue Port. It also shows how the
ADVAL statement is read.

```
 10 REM Listing 4.1
 20 MODE 1
 30 PROCinitialise
 40 REPEAT
 50 FOR channel=1 TO 4
 60 PROCadval(channel)
 70 NEXT channel
 80 UNTIL 0
 90 END
100 :
110 DEFPROCinitialise
120 X%=0:Y%=13:A%=10:D=&D00
130 VDU19,0,2,0,0,0
140 VDU19,1,5,0,0,0
150 VDU19,2,4,0,0,0
160 VDU19,3,0,0,0,0
170 VDU23;8202;0;0;0;
180 COLOUR 1
190 PROCdouble("The  Analogue  Port",10,1)
200 COLOUR 2
210 PROCdouble("Channel 1 ...",10,7)
220 PROCdouble("Channel 2 ...",10,14)
230 PROCdouble("Channel 3 ...",10,21)
240 PROCdouble("Channel 4 ...",10,28)
250 COLOUR 3
260 ENDPROC
270 :
280 DEFPROCadval(Ch)
290 value$=STR$(ADVAL(Ch))
300 IF value$="65520" THEN value$=" "
310 value$=value$+"    "
320 PROCdouble(value$,24,Ch*7)
330 ENDPROC
340 :
350 DEFPROCdouble(A$,x,y)
360 C$=CHR$(240)+CHR$8+CHR$10+CHR$(241)
370 FOR N=1 TO LEN(A$)
380 B$=MID$(A$,N,1)
390 ?D=ASC(B$)
400 CALL&FFF1
410 VDU23,240,D?1,D?1,D?2,D?2,D?3,D?3,D?4,D?4
420 VDU23,241,D?5,D?5,D?6,D?6,D?7,D?7,D?8,D?8
430 PRINT TAB(x+N-1,y)C$
440 NEXT N
450 ENDPROC
```

Description of program

The program works in mode 1, and displays the values of
the four channels in double-height print.

PROCinitialise sets the values for X%, Y%, A% and D.
These are required by the double-height procedure. This
procedure was used in chapter 3, and its method of
operation is described there. PROCinitialise also
redefines the four colours used on the screen, prints
the title in cyan, and prints channel 1-4 in blue. Once
this information has been printed on the screen, the

program enters an infinite loop between lines 40 and 80. This repeatedly cycles through the four channels, reads the analogue value for that channel and stores it as the string value$. It is then printed in double height. Because of the 1 Mohm resistor fitted between the +5 volt line and the analogue input, any of the four channels not connected to some sensor will give the value 65520. Line 300 filters out a reading of 65520 and prints a space instead to indicate that that channel is either out of range or has no sensing device connected.

CONNECTING A POTENTIOMETER

Potentiometers are variable resistors. They are frequently used in electronics and come in many shapes and sizes. They are used, for example, as volume and tone controls in audio amplifiers. For this application, any potentiometer with a spindle and a linear resistance in the range 1 Kohm to 100 Kohm can be used. Some potentiometers have a logarithmic track; they can be tried out but are of little use for most applications here. The linearity of potentiometers is

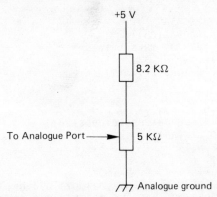

Figure 4.4   Circuit diagram for a potentiometer

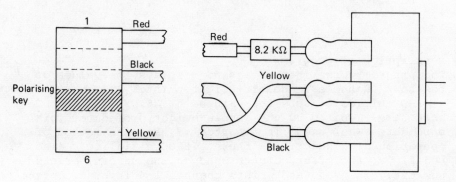

Figure 4.5 Wiring diagram for a potentiometer

never very good; but wirewound potentiometers are usually much better in this respect, but they are consequently more expensive. See figures 4.4 and 4.5.

Components required

1	Potentiometer 5 Kohms
1	Resistor 8.2 Kohms
1	6-way Minicon socket housing
3	Minicon terminals
1	Minicon polarising key
60 cm	Hook-up wire red
60 cm	Hook-up wire black
60 cm	Hook-up wire yellow

Construction
Strip and tin both ends of each piece of hook-up wire and solder or crimp one end of each wire to a Minicon terminal. Fit the red wire to position 1, the black to position 3 and the yellow to position 6. Fit the polarising key to position 4. Solder the resistor to one of the end solder tags of the potentiometer, and solder the red lead to the other end of the resistor. Solder the black lead to the other end terminal of the potentiometer, and finally solder the yellow wire to the centre terminal. Check the connections, then test the potentiometer by plugging it into the mother board and using listing 4.1. It is possible to use other resistance values for the potentiometer, and the resistor should be altered in proportion to keep a maximum voltage of 1.8 volts at the potentiometer. The program listing in appendix 1 will calculate the resistance required.

Uses of the potentiometer
The potentiometer is a device which can be used to convert rotary motion into an electrical signal that the computer can read through the Analogue Port. For some applications the rotary motion can prove to be a restriction, and a method of converting linear motion into a signal that the computer can process would be more useful. This can be done using a slider-potentiometer. This type of potentiometer will generally offer about 5 cm of travel, but they are difficult to find with wirewound tracks, and hence are not generally accurate enough for the purpose required here. The rotary motion of a normal potentiometer can be converted into a linear motion by one of two methods. The first involves purchasing a cord drum, which will fasten on to the spindle of the

potentiometer, and several cord guides. These are used in radio sets to move the pointer across the tuning scale. A similar arrangement can be used to convert a linear motion into a rotary motion.

A simpler method is to make an arm which can be attached to the spindle of the potentiometer. Provided that the movement at the end of the arm is small, it is a useful method of converting linear motion to rotary motion. An easy material to construct an arm from is Perspex. For this application, the Perspex should be at least 6.5 mm thick. The pointer should be about 24 cm long and 2 cm wide. Two small holes should be drilled 20 cm apart; one of these should then be enlarged to 6.35 mm to take the potentiometer spindle. The hard part is to drill a hole from the side of the arm to the centre of the larger hole, which can then be tapped to provide a method of fixing on to the spindle. As an alternative the arm could be glued on to the spindle using an epoxy adhesive. Before fixing the arm, the potentiometer should be fastened to a board, which can then be mounted either vertically or horizontally.

Listing 4.2 is a short demonstration program to show how the computer can convert the analogue signal into a distance. The system needs to be calibrated before it can be used. The arm assembly will need calibration marks for this. The board on which the arm is mounted should have a straight line drawn through the centre of the potentiometer fixing hole (see figure 4.6). Then an arc can be drawn on the board with a pencil placed in the small hole at the end of the arm. This arc should extend about 10 cm either side of the straight line, as shown in figure 4.6. A point 5 cm either side of the straight line should be marked which will be used for calibration. The accuracy of the final system will depend in part on the accuracy of these marks and also on the accuracy of the 20 cm holes in the arm.

When the marks have been placed on the board, the arm can be calibrated. This is done by finding the change in the ADVAL readings between the two known points, and halving this distance. The angle through which the arm will have moved is given by

$$SIN(angle) = \frac{length\ of\ opposite\ side}{length\ of\ hypotenuse}$$

The length of the opposite side is 5 cm and the length of the hypotenuse is 20 cm (the arm length). The angle is related to the ADVAL reading by the following equation

$$angle = change\ in\ ADVAL\ reading\ x\ constant$$

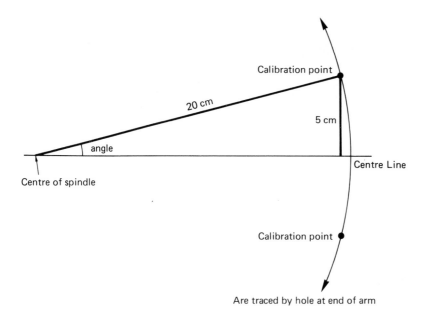

Figure 4.6   The geometry of the arm

Line 270 of listing 4.2 calculates this constant C, where ´upperlimit´ and ´lowerlimit´ are the two ADVAL readings taken at calibration. ´midpoint´ is the calculated ADVAL reading for the centre line; readings below this line will appear negative, those above will appear positive. The final distance is calculated in line 340, and the result will be in millimetres. The INT statement is used here to give the result to the nearest millimetre. This is about as accurate as the arm will measure. Because the result is to be in millimetres, the arm length must be in millimetres too.

```
 10 REM Listing 4.2
 20 PROCinitialise
 30 PROCcalibrate
 40 REPEAT
 50 PROCrun
 60 UNTIL 0
 70 END
 80 :
 90 DEFPROCinitialise
100 *FX16,1
110 @%=2
120 CLS
130 VDU23;8202;0;0;0;
140 ENDPROC
150 :
160 DEFPROCcalibrate
170 PRINT"Move pointer to mark 5 cm above line"
180 PROCspace
```

```
190 PROCadval
200 upperlimit=A%
210 I=INKEY(50)
220 PRINT"Move pointer to mark 5 cm below line"
230 PROCspace
240 PROCadval
250 lowerlimit=A%
260 midpoint=lowerlimit+(upperlimit-lowerlimit)/2
270 C=(ASN(5/20))*2/(upperlimit-lowerlimit)
280 CLS
290 ENDPROC
300 :
310 DEFPROCrun
320 PRINTTAB(5,5)"Distance is ";
330 PROCadval
340 PRINT INT(200*SIN(C*(A%-midpoint)));" mm"
350 ENDPROC
360 :
370 DEFPROCspace
380 SOUND 1,-15,60,5
390 PRINT'"Press space when ready"'
400 REPEAT
410 UNTIL GET=32
420 SOUND 1,-15,120,5
430 ENDPROC
440 :
450 DEFPROCadval
460 A%=0
470 FOR N=1 TO 25
480 A%=A%+ADVAL(1)
490 NEXT N
500 A%=A%/25
510 ENDPROC
```

A LIGHT-DEPENDENT RESISTOR

There are several types of light sensor available which
can be used by the Analogue Port. The simplest is a
light-dependent resistor (see figures 4.7 and 4.8).
This is a cadmium sulphide photoconductive cell, often
used in light-meters. The resistance changes from 1
Mohm in the dark to 200 ohms in strong light.
Connecting it to the mother board is easy; wire one
side to the analogue input, and the other side to the 0
volt pin (pin 3). A voltage divider is created because
of the 1 Mohm resistor already present on the mother
board. It does not matter which way round the
light-dependent resistor is wired. As the resistance
decreases with increasing light, the more light that
falls on the resistor the lower will be the ADVAL
reading.

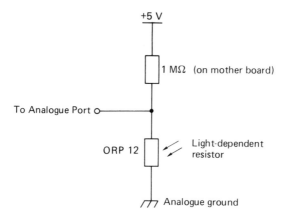

Figure 4.7 Circuit diagram for light-dependent resistor

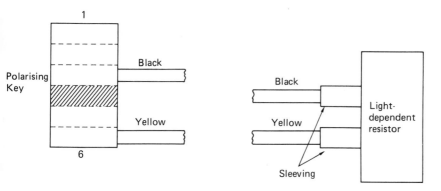

Figure 4.8 Wiring diagram for light-dependent resistor

Components required

1		Light-dependent resistor ORP12 or equivalent
1		6-way Minicon socket housing
2		Minicon terminals
1		Minicon polarising key
60 cm		Hook-up wire black
60 cm		Hook-up wire yellow
		Insulating sleeving

Construction

Strip and tin both ends of each piece of hook-up wire and solder one end to a Minicon terminal. Fit the black to position 3 and the yellow to position 6. Fit the polarising key to position 4. Solder the other ends of the wires to the light-dependent resistor. Use the sleeving to cover the solder connections. It should be slid on to the wires before soldering is started. As an alternative, electrical tape can be used to insulate the solder connections. Again plug into the mother board and use the test program. The reading should change as the resistor is pointed at a strong light. Do not expect, however, that it will operate over the full range of ADVAL values as did the potentiometer.

A PHOTOTRANSISTOR

Phototransistors are transistors that can be switched on and off by light falling on the transistor chip itself. Such transistors have a metal or plastic case with a window in the top. The more expensive versions have a lens. Phototransistors are more expensive than light-dependent resistors, but respond to a change in light much faster. If the phototransistor is wired up as in figure 4.9, then the ADVAL reading will decrease as the light intensity increases. The pre-set potentiometer allows the sensitivity of the sensor to be altered. This is useful if different photo-transistors from those specified are used.

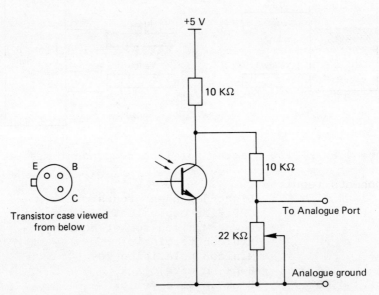

Figure 4.9   Circuit diagram for phototransistor

Components required

1 piece	0.1 Veroboard 12 tracks by 24 holes
1	Phototransistor type BPX25 or ZMX140 or similar
2	Resistors 10 Kohms
1	Pre-set potentiometer 22 Kohms
1	6-way 0.1 pitch Minicon socket (right-angled)

```
1              Minicon polarising key
2              Veropins
60 cm          Hook-up wire black
60 cm          Hook-up wire yellow
               Sleeving
```

Construction

Solder the black lead to the emitter of the transistor. Fit a sleeve over the solder joint. Solder the yellow wire to the collector and sleeve it too. The base wire of the transistor can be cut off. The lead connections for the phototransistor are shown in figure 4.9, but can vary with different case styles. If in doubt, check the connections in an electronics catalogue. The small Veroboard with the Minicon socket soldered at the bottom is the same as that used in chapter 3 for some of the small modules. On to this board the three resistors can be soldered, together with the two leads from the phototransistor. To test the circuit use listing 4.1. It should operate over almost the full ADVAL range, although it is unlikely that the ADVAL reading will go right down to 0.

Listing 4.3 will display the light level falling on the phototransistor pictorially. In addition, it shows some of the Analogue Port programming techniques that can be used. It can also be used with the light-dependent resistor.

```
 10 REM Listing 4.3
 20 *FX16,1
 30 MODE 5
 40 PROCdrawscreen
 50 REPEAT
 60 PROCrun
 70 UNTIL 0
 80 END
 90 :
100 DEFPROCdrawscreen
110 VDU23;8202;0;0;0;
120 VDU19,0,4,0,0,0
130 VDU19,3,0,0,0,0
140 COLOUR 2
150 PRINTTAB(4,1)"LIGHT SENSOR"
160 PRINTTAB(2,5)"Plug sensor into"
170 PRINTTAB(5,6)"channel  1"
180 FOR N=0 TO 20 STEP 4
190 MOVE 120-N,300-N:DRAW 1156+N,300-N
200 DRAW 1156+N,600+N:DRAW 120-N,600+N
210 DRAW 120-N,300-N
220 NEXT N
230 PRINTTAB(0,24)"Dark            Light"
240 COLOUR 1
250 A%=128
260 ENDPROC
```

```
270 :
280 DEFPROCrun
290 oldA%=A%
300 PROCadval
310 GCOL0,129
320 IF A%>oldA% THEN VDU24,oldA%;304;A%;596;16
330 GCOL0,128
340 IF A%<oldA% THEN VDU24,A%;304;oldA%;596;16
350 ENDPROC
360 :
370 DEFPROCadval
380 A%=0
390 FOR N=1 TO 100
400 *FX17,1
410 A%=A%+(ADVAL(1) DIV 64)
420 NEXT N
430 A%=128+1024-(A%/100)
440 ENDPROC
```

*FX16,1 at line 20 is the command to select only
channel 1 to be sampled. PROCdrawscreen sets up the
screen display. Lines 50 to 70 are an infinite loop to
call up the procedure PROCrun; this is the procedure
that reads the value at the Analogue Port and displays
it as a red bar on the screen. Line 110 switches off
the cursor, line 120 changes the background colour to
blue, and line 130 changes colour 3 to black. Lines 180
to 220 draw a thick rectangular box in black inside
which the red bar proportional in length to the voltage
sensed by the Analogue Port will be displayed. This
voltage will be a function of the light intensity
falling on the sensor. (Note that this function will
not be linear.) Lines 280 to 350 take the ADVAL reading
and convert it to the red bar. This is done by defining
a graphics window the same size as the bar to be drawn
(line 320), or by reducing the size of the bar if
necessary (line 330), and then clearing the screen in
red in the former case, or in blue in the latter case.
This avoids having the whole display flickering.

The Analogue Port is sampled by the procedure
PROCadval. Inside the procedure, a conversion of
channel 1 is first forced, then the value is summed.
The value is divided by 64 to convert it to the range
of the screen graphics (0 to 1023). The Analogue Port
is sampled 100 times and then the summation is divided
by 100. This not only gives a greater accuracy, but it
slows the program down to avoid the bar giving too
jerky a display. (Try the effect of not sampling the
ADVAL reading 100 times.)

Using the light sensor
The obvious use of the light sensor is for reading

ambient light levels. However, if a fixed light source
is available then a range of other control applications
can be explored. A good light source is a LED. This
uses little power and can operate from the +5 volt line
from the Analogue Port with a suitable resistor to
limit the current; it can be plugged into a spare
channel socket. If the light sensor is fixed opposite
the light source, then the computer will be able to
detect anything crossing the light path. It could even
form a crude smoke sensor.

   If the light sensor is placed next to the light
source and both are pointing in the same direction, the
sensor will be able to respond when placed in front of
a reflecting surface. Hence it could be used to
differentiate between dull and shiny objects. Lastly,
if a strong white light source is available, the
phototransistor is sensitive enough to differentiate
between different levels of reflected light from
coloured objects.

A THERMISTOR

A thermistor is a resistor with a resistance that
varies with temperature. There are several types
available: rod thermistors, glass-encased thermistors,
disc thermistors and bead thermistors. They range in
price from a few pence to several pounds. For sensing
temperature changes, bead thermistors are the best
because of their small physical size. They are able to
respond quickly to changes in temperature. The main
problem with thermistors is the difficulty of
calculating the temperature from a known resistance.

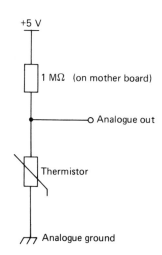

Figure 4.10   Circuit diagram for thermistor

They are suitable for simply indicating changes in temperature. For accurate readings it is better to use the temperature-sensing integrated circuit described next and shown in figure 4.10. The thermistor forms a voltage divider with the 1 Mohm resistor mounted on the mother board.

Components required

1		Bead thermistor
1		6-way Minicon socket housing
2		Minicon terminals
1		Minicon polarising key
60 cm		Hook-up wire black
60 cm		Hook-up wire yellow
		Sleeving

Construction
Strip and tin both ends of each piece of hook-up wire and solder, or crimp, one end of each to a Minicon terminal. Fit the black to position 3 and the yellow to position 6. Fit the polarising key to position 4. Slide a sleeve on to each wire. Solder the other ends of the wires to the thermistor. Use the sleeving to cover the solder connections. As an alternative, electrical tape can be used to insulate the solder connections. Again plug into the mother board and use the test program. The thermistor will not give a reading over the full ADVAL range of values.

A PRECISION TEMPERATURE SENSOR
In many respects the thermistor is not an ideal device for simple temperature measurements. It is not linear, the mathematics are complicated, and the device needs calibrating first. There is a cheap temperature sensor chip on the market that is linear, runs from a +5 volt supply and needs no calibration. This chip is the LM335Z precision temperature sensor. It requires a minimum of components to function with the BBC microcomputer's Analogue Port. It has an output voltage of 3.00 volts at 27°C and a temperature change of 10 mV for every °C. It has a maximum calibration error of 2°C and can be calibrated to give an error of less than 1°C. It operates over the range -10°C to 100°C, and can be used up to 125°C for short periods.

To reduce the voltage output down to a level that can be read by the Analogue Port, a simple divide-by-three resistor network is used.

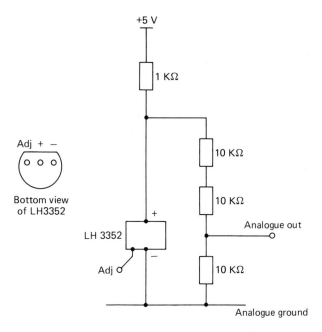

Figure 4.11   Circuit diagram for temperature sensor

Components required

1		Integrated circuit LM335Z precision temperature sensor
3		10 Kohm resistors
1		1 Kohm resistor
1	piece	0.1 Veroboard 24 holes by 12 tracks
1		6-pin Minicon socket
1		Minicon polarising key
2		Veroboard pins
60	cm	Hook-up wire black
60	cm	Hook-up wire yellow
		Sleeving

Construction
As there are four resistors to be wired into the circuit, they are first mounted on a Veroboard daughter board. The board is fitted with a Minicon socket, and the components and Veroboard pins are fitted and soldered into position; then the sensor is wired to the board using the hook-up cable. Construction is straightforward, but remember that the solder connections at the sensor must be insulated with sleeving to avoid short-circuits. As the adjust lead is not required, it can be cut off at the base of the IC.

A temperature graph program

Listing 4.4 is a real-time program to graph the temperature against time. The time axis has automatic scaling. When the graph is completed, the graph is redrawn, but the time continues. It can be restarted by pressing ESCAPE. The precision temperature sensor must be used for this program, and it must be plugged into channel 1.

```
 10 REM Listing 4.4
 20 ON ERROR RUN
 30 MODE1
 40 TIME=-100:temp=20:@%=0
 50 REPEAT
 60 PROCsetscreen
 70 PROCrun
 80 UNTIL 0
 90 END
100 :
110 DEFPROCsetscreen
120 CLS
130 VDU23;8202;0;0;0;
140 VDU19,0,4,0,0,0
150 COLOUR 2
160 PRINTTAB(5,1)"GRAPH OF TEMPERATURE AGAINST TIME"
170 COLOUR 3
180 MOVE 120,120:DRAW1280,120
190 MOVE 140,120:DRAW140,1024
200 VDU28,0,12,0,0
210 PRINT"TEMPERATURE"
220 VDU26,5
230 FOR N=0 TO 8
240 MOVE 120,120+100*N:DRAW 140,120+100*N
250 MOVE 40,132+100*N
260 PRINTN*10
270 NEXT N
280 VDU 4
290 PRINTTAB(28,31)"TIME (sec)";
300 ENDPROC
310 :
320 DEFPROCrun
330 FOR X=140 TO 1200 STEP 4
340 Y%=0
350 FOR T=1 TO 100
360 IF TIME MOD 3000<10 PROCtime
370 Y%=Y%+ADVAL(1)
380 NEXT T
390 Y%=Y%/100
400 temp=(Y%*1.8*3*100/65536)-273
410 IF X=140 THEN MOVE X,120+temp*10
420 DRAW X,120+temp*10
430 NEXT X
440 ENDPROC
450 :
460 DEFPROCtime
470 VDU5
```

```
480 t$=STR$(TIME DIV 100)
490 x=(LEN(t$))*16
500 MOVE X-x,72
510 PRINT t$
520 MOVE X,100:DRAW X,120
530 MOVE X,120+temp*10
540 VDU4
550 ENDPROC
```

DEFPROCsetscreen lays out the axes of the graph and labels them. DEFPROCrun is the main part of the program where the Analogue Port is read and graphed on the screen. The Analogue Port is summed 100 times, during which line 360 keeps an eye on the time so that every 30 seconds it can print the time on the axis using PROCtime. Line 400 converts the Analogue Port value to a temperature. The circuit divides the voltage at the output by 3 to suit the analogue-to-digital converter; hence the analogue value is multiplied by 3. The value of 273 is subtracted to convert the temperature from degrees Kelvin to degrees Celsius.

DEFPROCtime is a procedure that prints the time on the screen every 30 seconds. A mark is also put below the X axis of the graph and the print is centred about this mark.

A MAGNETIC FIELD SENSOR

The magnetic field sensor is a linear output Hall-effect device type 634SS2. In comparison with other ICs used in this book it is rather expensive. It is a 4-lead device that operates off a 5 volt supply. There are two outputs, one of which increases in voltage with increasing gauss, and the other decreases in voltage with increasing gauss. Positive gauss represents the south pole of the magnet facing the sensing area. Using a 5 volt supply the output voltages for given field strengths are shown in figure 4.12. The voltages need to be dropped across a voltage divider in order to be within the range of the analogue-to-digital converter. The circuit diagram is shown in figure 4.13.

Field Strength	Output 1	Output 2
+1000	2.84	1.14
+600	2.47	1.52
+200	2.10	1.91
0	1.92	2.10
-200	1.74	2.48
-600	1.35	2.66
-1000	0.94	3.04

Figure 4.12   Output voltages

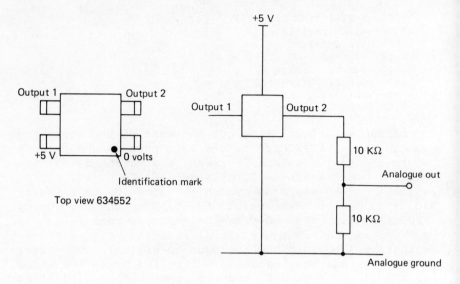

Figure 4.13   Circuit diagram for magnetic sensor

Components required

1		Integrated circuit 634SS2 linear output Hall-effect device
2		10 Kohm resistors
1	piece	0.1 Veroboard, 24 holes by 12 tracks
1		6-pin Minicon socket
1		Minicon polarising key
3		Veroboard pins
60	cm	Hook-up wire red
60	cm	Hook-up wire black
60	cm	Hook-up wire yellow

Construction

The magnetic sensor uses the same small daughter circuit board as the precision temperature sensor, and the construction is identical. It should be remembered that this circuit divides the output voltage from the sensor by 2 before it is converted by the analogue-to-digital converter, and any software using this circuit needs to take this into account. This device is sensitive over a range of only a few centimetres, unless very strong magnetic fields are present.

5 Using Lego for Control

Now that all the modules for the User Port and the Analogue Port have been introduced, they can be utilised to build examples of computer control. There are many such examples that could be built. However, just one application is described in this chapter in order to give the reader a starting point for developing his or her own ideas. This project is an integration of programming techniques, computer interfacing and model making that at first sight appears quite simple, but in practice requires thought and care if it is to work correctly. The difficulties are not those anticipated, and the project highlights the sorts of problem that are often encountered in automated systems. The project will be described in some detail in order to illustrate these difficulties and the methods used to overcome them. Some of the problems are overcome by improving the design, others by improving the software. Computer control is a fascinating area of computer usage because it greatly increases flexibility of operation, and allows changes in operation to be made more easily.

This project used Technical Lego to build a conveyor that will sort out a nominated coloured block (see figures 5.1 and 5.2). There are four common Lego colours: red, blue, white and yellow. Technical Lego is an ideal medium for such a project as it is a readily available modular construction kit that contains low-voltage motors that are easily connected to the system described in chapter 3. The motors are small but very powerful and are ideal for powering many projects. Technical Lego is also very versatile and remarkably strong, so that it can be used to construct many exciting projects.

This project is one that will require a fair amount of experimentation and patience if it is to work correctly. It could have been simplified just to count the number of blocks passing along a conveyor. It could then have been extended to try to record the different colours of each block passing along the conveyor.

The following modules are required

        Analogue Port mother board
        User Port mother board PB0-PB3
        Phototransistor sensor
        1-pole reed relay module
        2-pole changeover relay module

The Lego requirement is not easy to specify as there are numerous ways in which the project could have been built. However, the following special parts were needed to build the model shown in figure 5.1.

        Two 4.5 volt motor
        Two battery packs
        Lighting set (4.5 volt)
        Two gear blocks
        Lego technical set

A good assortment of rubber bands was found most useful too!

The sorter accepted a series of small Lego blocks, and the user was invited by the computer to select one of the four colours available. The coloured blocks were placed on a conveyor belt on the sorter. A phototransistor was used to sense the colour of the block as it passed along the conveyor. If the computer found a block of the colour specified, then it actuated a plunger which pushed the block into a separate bin. The other coloured blocks fell off the end of the conveyor into another bin.

THE THEORY
Sorting colours can be achieved using a phototransistor to measure the light reflected from a coloured surface. As a phototransistor is more sensitive to some coloured lights than to others if the differences are great enough then the computer is able to differentiate between them. If the items to be sorted are transparent, then the light can be passed through them rather than being reflected.

This can be tested using the phototransistor module described in chapter 4 together with listing 4.1. If different coloured filters are put in front of the phototransistor, then changes in the ADVAL reading will be seen. Similarly if light is reflected off coloured objects and picked up by a shielded phototransistor, then changes in the ADVAL reading should also be noticed.

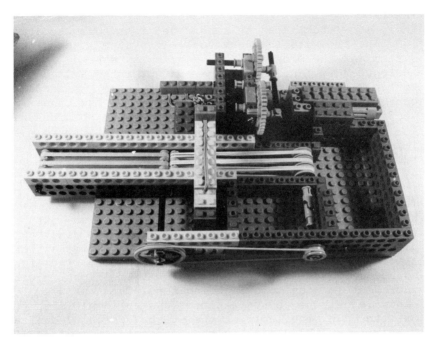

Figure 5.1   Photograph of colour sorter

Figure 5.2   Photograph of colour sorter

THE LEGO MODEL
The Lego model can be subdivided into three separate
modules. They are the conveyor belt system, the optical
system and the plunger. The light was sensed by the
Analogue Port, and the plunger was operated by the User
Port. The conveyor belt system requires no computer
control, although if required it could be switched on
and off by the computer. This facility is not included
in listing 5.1, but would be straightforward to
implement. An extra reed relay module would also be
required.

The optical system
When this system (figure 5.3) was first tried out it
relied on reflected light. The computer did show a
different reading when different coloured blocks were
placed in front of the phototransistor. The light
source used was one of the 4.5 volt light blocks
included in the Lego lighting sets. This was used for
convenience. The phototransistor was an ideal size to
fit through the hole of one of the special Technical
Lego bricks. The flange on the transistor fitted neatly
into the slightly larger groove round the hole. A slot
was cut in the top of the block to slip the wires
through, in order to avoid having to thread the block
on the lead before it was soldered to the
phototransistor. A second block placed in front neatly
held the phototransistor in position, and provided a
tube to make the phototransistor sensitive only to
light coming directly into the tube. The phototransistor was mounted adjacent to the light source and
placed at the side of the conveyor. This design proved
to be very simple to build and did indeed work, but
when the model was finished and tested it was found
that there was quite a large variation in the readings
observed for the same block. This was found to be due
to slight misalignment of the blocks so that the light
was not always reflected directly into the phototransistor. Hence it would not sort reliably. Also the
difference in the ADVAL readings between the four
colours was not sufficient to allow for slight changes
in each of the blocks.
    To get round these problems, transmitted light was
used instead. The light source was placed at the
opposite side of the conveyor so that the light had to
pass through the blocks. The exact position for the
light was found by experimentation in order to give the
best spread of ADVAL readings between the presence of
each of the blocks and the absence of a block. It was
found that if the light source was placed one brick

layer above the conveyor, this gave the best and most reliable spread of readings. Surprisingly enough, there was quite a change in the ADVAL readings, far larger than had occurred when using reflected light, and the repeatability of the system was good. There was an adequate repeatability, and a great enough range of readings between the different colours to enable the software to have a good error margin. On average, the repeatability was found to be within 2-3 units, and the closest pair of readings were separated by about 30 units. Hence a tolerance of 10 either side of the setting-up values was accepted.

Figure 5.3   Photograph of colour sensor system

The beauty of using Lego is that such experimentation is very easy and the project is then simple to alter and improve. With the light source and detector arrangement outlined above, that is, with the light passing through the block and not being reflected from the face of the block, the phototransistor is not detecting actual changes in colour but rather the changes between different densities of each coloured plastic. One problem soon encountered with this system was that the lighting block had to be brightly lit; and did not work well if the batteries were running down. There was an improvement when the lights were worked off their own power supply.

The conveyor
The conveyor belt carried the blocks past the phototransistor, past the plunger and into the bin at

the end of the conveyor. There were actually two
conveyor belts, the first running much slower than the
second. This was to spread the blocks out as they went
past the light system and the plunger. Otherwise there
was a danger of two blocks being pushed off the
conveyor together. It also meant that the software
could be kept simple. Without this refinement the
program would have had to keep track of several blocks
at once because of the physical distance that had to
exist between the detector and the plunger. Rather than
having to do this, it was easier to arrange that the
blocks were spaced out so that there was only one block
on the conveyor between the detector and the plunger at
any moment. In that way, once the computer program had
detected a coloured block of the selected colour, it
simply waited a pre-determined time before actuating
the plunger. This is an example of the way the physical
design goes hand in hand with the program design.

The conveyor system was made from Technical Lego
axles together with the small axle stops that made
ideal small-diameter pulleys. Three of the axle stops
were placed on each axle. This gave a conveyor width
that was just right for a 3 x 2 block to pass along
sideways. Then rubber bands were stretched across these
pulleys to form the conveyor belt. The length of the
conveyor depended on the length of the rubber bands
available. Two conveyors were needed, the first one
running at about a quarter the speed of the second.
This was achieved by using reduction gearing in the
drive from the first conveyor to the second. Both
conveyors were run from one Lego motor, suitably geared
down. Figures 5.1 and 5.2 show the layout of the two
conveyor belts.

The plunger

The plunger posed several problems. Was it possible to
have a plunger that, once actuated, would cycle round
and end at the same point? Would it work fast enough to
push the block off the conveyor? How could the timing
be worked out so that the correct brick was always hit?
Would the plunger be strong enough? In the end it was
decided to make a simple plunger that was moved out and
moved back again using separate computer signals. The
reason for this was that it was easy to construct a
Lego plunger with built-in end stops, and which would
require a double-pole changeover module for the motor
control, but far harder to ensure that a single-action
plunger returned back to its exact start position on
its own. The plunger design shown in figure 5.4 took

Figure 5.4 Photograph of the plunger

only one-fifth of a second to complete its cycle. At
such a speed the only reliable way to stop it at the
correct point was to use mechanical end stops. These
end stops can be seen on the inside of the two large
gear wheels. The plunger was axle-mounted on two gear
wheels to keep it horizontal. Both gear wheels were
driven from a small gear which was connected to the
motor by a rubber band and pulleys. The 2-pole
changeover switch module circuit is shown in figure
5.5. The relay is a 2-pole changeover type with a
voltage of 5-6 volts. DIL reed relays with a coil
resistance of over 300 ohms can be obtained, but they
tend to be expensive, so a miniature printed circuit
board mounting type was used instead. This had a coil
resistance of about 60 ohms, but was driven without
difficulty from the 7400 NAND gate. To improve
reliability, however, it is better to use a transistor
to drive the relay. Connect the base of a BC108 (or
equivalent transistor) through a 2.2 Kohm resistor to
the PB0 output, wiring one side of the relay coil to
the +5 volt line and the other side to the transistor
collector. The emitter of the transistor is connected
to the 0 volt line. The protection diode is still
needed across the coil to prevent damage to the driver
circuitry from back e.m.f.s. It would be possible to
drive the relay from a single-pole reed switch relay
instead.
    The wiring for the plunger motor is shown in figure
5.5.

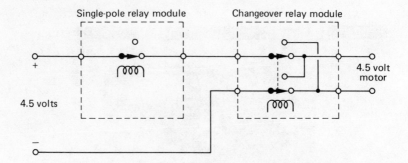

Figure 5.5   The plunger motor wiring

The software

The software was developed alongside the hardware and
was altered and improved by trial and error. The first
part of the program tested the various functions of the
sorter. The next part checked the ADVAL reading for
each coloured block in turn. This was found to be
essential because of variations in the light intensity.
Because this program will probably need to be altered
to suit individual needs, it is described in more
detail than many of the other programs in the book.


```
 10 REM Listing 5.1 Colour sorter
 20 MODE 1
 30 PROCinitialise
 40 PROCsetup
 50 PROCrun
 60 END
 70 :
 80 DEFPROCinitialise
 90 ?&FE62=&FF
100 ?&FE60=0
110 wait=550
120 *FX16,0
130 *FX11,0
140 DIM colour(4),colour$(4)
150 X%=0:Y%=13:A%=10:D=&D00
160 VDU19,0,4,0,0,0
170 VDU19,3,6,0,0,0
180 VDU23;8202;0;0;0;
190 PROCtitle
200 colour$(1)="BLUE"
210 colour$(2)="RED"
220 colour$(3)="WHITE"
230 colour$(4)="YELLOW"
240 ENDPROC
250 :
260 DEFPROCsetup
270 PROCdouble("Setting up",15,4)
280 COLOUR 2
```

```
290 PRINT´´"Connect up light and switch on"
300 PROCspace
310 REPEAT:UNTILGET=32
320 SOUND 1,-15,100,10
330 COLOUR 3
340 PRINTTAB(0,10)"Connect a phototransistor to
    channel 1"
350 PRINT"of the Analogue Port."
360 PRINT´"Test it now: "
370 PROCspace
380 COLOUR 1
390 REPEAT
400 PROCadval(1)
410 PRINTTAB(13,13)"     "
420 PRINTTAB(13,13);adval%
430 UNTIL INKEY(0)=32
440 SOUND 1,-15,100,10
450 COLOUR 2
460 PRINT´´"Put a on/off relay in position PB0."
470 PRINT"Put a changeover relay in position PB1."
480 PRINT"Wire up so that PB0 switches motor on"
490 PRINT"and off again, and PB1 reverses the"
500 PRINT"direction."
510 PRINT"Press ´O´ to move the plunger out,"
520 PRINT"press ´I´ to move the plunger in."
530 REPEAT
540 A$=GET$
550 IF A$="O" THEN PROCuserout(1,"on"):
    PROCuserout(0,"on"): I=INKEY(10):
PROCuserout(0,"off"):
    PROCuserout(1,"off")
560 IF A$="I" THEN PROCuserout(0,"on"): I=INKEY(10):
    PROCuserout(0,"off")
570 UNTIL A$=" "
580 PROCuserout(0,"on"):I=INKEY(10):
    PROCuserout(0,"off")
590 SOUND 1,-15,100,10
600 PROCtitle
610 PRINTTAB(0,9)"Place bricks on conveyor"
620 PRINT"in the following order:"´
630 COLOUR 2
640 FOR n=1 TO 4
650 PRINTTAB(10)colour$(n)
660 NEXT n
670 COLOUR 3
680 PRINT´"Start conveyor."
690 PROCspace
700 REPEAT:UNTIL GET=32:CLS
710 PROCtitle
720 PROCdouble("Finding reading for each colour",5,4)
730 COLOUR 2
740 PROCadval(1)
750 test%=adval%
760 C%=1
770 REPEAT
780 PROCadval(1)
790 IF adval%<test%+25 THEN GOTO870
800 REPEAT
```

```
 810 PROCadval(1)
 820 IF colour(C%)<adval% THEN colour(C%)=adval%
 830 UNTIL adval%<test%+25
 840 PROCdouble(colour$(C%)+" ... "+
     STR$(colour(C%)),5,4*(C%+1))
 850 C%=C%+1
 860 I=INKEY(500)
 870 UNTIL C%=5
 880 SOUND 1,-15,100,10
 890 PRINT´´"Are these OK?"SPC(62);
 900 IF GET$="N" THEN CLS:GOTO 600
 910 PROCtitle
 920 COLOUR 2
 930 PRINTTAB(10,8)"Select colour B/R/W/Y ";
 940 COLOUR 3
 950 C%=INSTR("BRWY",GET$)
 960 IF C%=0 THEN GOTO 950
 970 PRINTTAB(10,8)SPC(22)
 980 PROCdouble("Sorting "+colour$(C%) +
     " bricks    ",10,4)
 990 ENDPROC
1000 :
1010 DEFPROCrun
1020 REPEAT
1030 PROCadval(1)
1040 IF (colour(C%)-adval%)<25 THEN PROCcheck
1050 PROCdouble("            ",10,16)
1060 UNTIL 0
1070 ENDPROC
1080 :
1090 DEFPROCadval(channel)
1100 adval%=0
1110 FOR N=1 TO 25
1120 *FX17,1
1130 adval%=adval%+ADVAL(channel)DIV 32
1140 NEXT N
1150 adval%=adval%/25
1160 ENDPROC
1170 :
1180 DEFPROCdouble(A$,x,y)
1190 C$=CHR$(240)+CHR$8+CHR$10+CHR$(241)
1200 FOR N=1 TO LEN(A$)
1210 B$=MID$(A$,N,1)
1220 ?D=ASC(B$)
1230 CALL&FFF1
1240 VDU23,240,D?1,D?1,D?2,D?2,D?3,D?3,D?4,D?4
1250 VDU23,241,D?5,D?5,D?6,D?6,D?7,D?7,D?8,D?8
1260 PRINT TAB(x+N-1,y)C$
1270 NEXT N
1280 ENDPROC
1290 :
1300 DEFPROCuserout(channel,state$)
1310 val=2^channel
1320 IF (?&FE62 AND val)=0 THEN ?&FE62=?&FE62+val
1330 IF state$="on" AND (?&FE60 AND val)=0 THEN
     ?&FE60=?&FE60+val
1340 IF state$="off" AND (?&FE60 AND val)=val THEN
     ?&FE60=?&FE60-val
```

```
1350 ENDPROC
1360 :
1370 DEFPROCpush
1380 I=INKEY(wait)
1390 PROCuserout(1,"on")
1400 PROCuserout(0,"on")
1410 I=INKEY(10)
1420 PROCuserout(1,"off")
1430 I=INKEY(10)
1440 PROCuserout(0,"off")
1450 ENDPROC
1460 :
1470 DEFPROCcheck
1480 check=0
1490 REPEAT
1500 PROCadval(1)
1510 IF check<adval% THEN check=adval%
1520 UNTIL adval%<test%+25
1530 IF ABS(colour(C%)-check)>10 THEN ENDPROC
1540 SOUND 1,-15,125,10
1550 PROCdouble(colour$(C%)+" FOUND",10,16)
1560 PROCpush
1570 ENDPROC
1580 :
1590 DEFPROCspace
1600 VDU24,175;10;1100;60;5,18,0,131,12,18,0,0
1610 MOVE200,47:PRINT"Press space bar to continue"
1620 *FX15,0
1630 VDU4,18,0,128,18,0,3,26
1640 ENDPROC
1650 :
1660 DEFPROCtitle
1670 CLS
1680 COLOUR 1
1690 PROCdouble("Testing for Colours",11,1)
1700 COLOUR 3
1710 ENDPROC
```

Description of program

30   PROCinitialise is the procedure in which all the variables are defined, arrays dimensioned and the actual screen colours defined.

40   PROCsetup is the procedure that allows the various functions of the colour sorter to be tested. This facility is most useful when the Lego model is being built, as it avoids writing separate routines to test each of the functions in turn. This procedure also takes a sample reading of each block from the Analogue Port so that it is later able to 'recognise' each block.

50   PROCrun is the procedure that checks each block in turn and actuates the plunger when it finds the block of the selected colour. This procedure could be extended considerably. It allows the user to choose only one block, but it could easily choose more than one colour, count how many blocks of each colour are passed along the conveyor, and allow the selected colour to be changed. It could also be used to allow only a pre-determined number of blocks of the specified colour to be sorted. There are many alternatives that can be programmed according to user requirements.

90   This sets all 8 bits of the User Port to output.

100   This sets each bit of the User Port to 0.

110   'wait' is the variable that determines the length of time between recognition of a block to be sorted and actuation of the plunger. This is put at the start of the program because it needs to be altered to suit the speed and length of the particular conveyor constructed. This variable could be determined in PROCsetup by the inclusion of a routine to time the delay, but this has not been done because it did not need to be too precise in the project described, and setting-up time was saved.

120   This switches off the analogue-to-digital conversions. When channel 1 needs to be read, it can be forced using *FX17,1. This speeds up the conversion rate, which is important in this application.

130   This switches off the keyboard auto-repeat.

140   This dimensions two arrays, 'colour' and 'colour$'. 'colour' stores the test ADVAL reading for each block, and 'colour$' is the string array to store the name of the colour. This saves programming time later, as the colours will need to be printed on the screen quite frequently.

150   These are defined for the double-height procedure which is described in chapter 3.

160   This defines the background colour to be blue.

170   This defines colour 3, which in mode 1 is white, to be cyan.

180   This switches off the cursor.

190   PROCtitle is the procedure to print the title of the program in double height at the top of the screen in red.

200-240   This defines the four colours to be used.

270   PROCdouble is the procedure to print double height on the screen. Three parameters need to be defined. The first is the text to be printed in double height, the second and third are the X and Y text co-ordinates of the first letter.

300   PROCspace is a procedure to print the ´Press space bar to continue´ message at the bottom of the screen.

310   This loop will repeat until the space bar, which has an ASCII value of 32, is pressed.

320   This sounds a note to indicate that the space bar has been pressed.

400   PROCadval is the procedure to read the Analogue Port and return a value in the integer variable ´adval%´.

410-420   These two lines first clear the previous reading then print the latest Analogue Port reading on the screen. This section of the program enables the light sensor to be tested.

550-560   These two lines allow the plunger to be moved out using the ´O´ key and in using the ´I´ key, and hence test whether or not the plunger is working correctly. The User Port is programmed in the procedure PROCuserout. The two parameters specify the bit of the port to be programmed and the state of the bit. This has been specified using ´on´ and ´off´ to make the program easier to understand. Bit 0 controls the on/off function of the plunger, and bit 1 the polarity reversal for the plunger motor. The time delay introduced using the INKEY statement might need altering for different plunger mechanisms.

580   This line returns the plunger to its return position, as it is possible to leave the plunger test section with the plunger out across the conveyor.

610-900   This routine takes a sample reading of each of the four colours, which the program is then able to use as a reference. The sample readings are stored in the array ´colour´. First, however, a sample reading is taken for the light sensor when no block is in front of the conveyor. This value is stored in the variable ´test%´. The Analogue Port is repeatedly sampled, until the reading goes a pre-defined amount above this empty conveyor reading. In this case the pre-defined amount is set at 25 (line 790); however, this might need changing to suit the particular light sensor used. If this amount is exceeded then it means that a block is passing in front of the sensor, and the highest reading recorded as the block passes the sensor is retained. This was found to be the most reliable way of recording a value for a block. Then the value for that block is printed on the screen. Lastly, the user has the choice of accepting the range of values recorded, or of repeating the test. The test will need to be repeated if the values of two of the blocks are so similar that the computer will not be able to differentiate between them. It is also useful initially to repeat the test several times and record each set of results to find out how repeatable the results are. If there is a wide variation, then either the Lego model needs improving or the allowed tolerance needs changing.

930-960   These lines input the colour to be sorted. This is a part of the program that could be extended as indicated earlier.

980   This prints which colour brick is to be sorted.

1010-1070 This is the main procedure. It constantly checks the light sensor reading, and if a significant change is seen then control passes to the procedure PROCcheck. This procedure then checks which brick is passing the sensor, waits a pre-determined time, and actuates the plunger if the brick is ´recognised´.

1090-1160 This procedure reads the Analogue Port. The port is read 25 times to reduce errors. It does it by first forcing a reading on channel 1 at line 1120, and then taking only the most significant part of the reading.

1180-1280 This procedure prints the text defined in the first parameter in double height. It has already been described in chapter 3.

1300-1350 This procedure first sets the appropriate bit to output, and then switches that bit on or off as required. The procedure checks to see that the bit is not already set or cleared before making any changes, thus avoiding other bits being altered. Line 1320 is not necessary in this program, but is included in this general-purpose routine. A similar routine could be written to configure and read bits of the User Port when set to input.

1370-1450 This procedure controls the operation of the plunger.First there is a wait period to ensure that the block is in front of the plunger. Then the plunger is actuated, next the changeover relay is actuated, and the plunger then returns to its rest position.

1470-1570 This routine is very similar to the test routine described above. Indeed this must be so, otherwise there is likely to be a discrepancy between these readings and the test readings, and the system will not then select the correct blocks. The procedure also prints a message on the screen when it finds the selected block. It could be extended to print the colour of all the blocks that it detects. Having detected the selected coloured block, the procedure then passes control to PROCpush in order for the plunger to be activated. Line 1530 is the critical line. The highest recorded reading is stored in the variable ´check´. This reading is then tested against the test reading for the selected colour, and if the difference is less than 10, the block is ´recognised´. The tolerance of 10 might well need to be altered, depending on the repeatability of the system, and the spread of readings between each of the blocks.

1590-1640 This procedure defines a graphics window and reverses the colours to print the space bar message at the bottom of the screen. *FX15,0 clears the keyboard buffer to prevent earlier key presses being used.

6   Building a Graphics Tablet

A graphics tablet is a device that draws pictures on the computer screen. Normally the drawing of complex pictures on the screen is a tedious task. To draw an outline of a map requires the plotting of several hundred points. The graphics tablet described in this chapter is able to draw such an outline in a matter of minutes. It also illustrates an application of some of the techniques covered earlier in the book, and shows how an uncomplicated device together with versatile software can be combined together to produce a useful tool.

The graphics tablet has the following commands

L	Line drawing	Sloping Horizontal Vertical Solid or dotted
R	Rectangle drawing	Solid or dotted
C	Circle drawing	Any regular polygon from 3-sided to what appears as a circle Solid or dotted
F	Follow mode	A trace following the positions of the pointer, will appear on the screen
I	Infill	Single-colour or multi- colour infilling of any shape
D	Define	Defines which colours to use
A	Alter	Alters drawing colour
X	Load	Loads in new picture

S	Save	Saves existing picture
P	Print	Prints on screen Horizontal or vertical Double height
W	Wipe	Wipes the screen clear
X	Dump	Dumps picture to printer

The tablet will work in any graphics mode, and also allows the user to have user-defined characters. This enables such things as electronic symbols to be defined and included in pictures. The software is in two parts. The first part calibrates the tablet. This means that there is no complicated setting up of the tablet when it is being built. The first program also contains a character definer, so that defined characters can then be used in the second part of the program. The second program is the program that contains all the drawing routines listed above and displays the picture as it is drawn. The tablet is so designed that wire movement is kept to a minimum; this prevents the arm feeling stiff and minimises wire breakage. The finished tablet is shown in figure 6.1.

Figure 6.1   Photograph of finished tablet

Materials required

The materials required are all easy to obtain, the most difficult probably being the wirewound potentiometers. The better the quality of potentiometer the better the graphics tablet will work. It is no use using the normal carbon track potentiometer listed in catalogues and found in electronics shops; they are not linear enough.

1 piece	Perspex 48 cm by 40 cm by 6.4 mm thick
1 piece	Perspex 24 cm by 4 cm by 6.4 mm thick
1 piece	Perspex 23 cm by 4 cm by 6.4 mm thick
1	15-pin ´D type´ connector
1	15-pin ´D type´ connector cover
1	Resistor 2.7 Kohms
1	Electrolytic capacitor 10 μF 16 V
2	5 Kohm wirewound potentiometers (with at least 25 mm spindles)
2	30 mm aluminium knobs
1.5 m	4-core cable
1	5 mm ´P´ clip
1	12 mm by M3 bolt
1	M3 washer
1	M3 nut
1	Small piece of felt
	Epoxy resin

Construction

Construction of the tablet is not too difficult and a minimum of tools is required. If care is taken during construction to keep measurements accurate, then the finished tablet will be quite accurate. First cut the pieces of Perspex to size and drill them as shown in figures 6.2 to 6.4. Perspex is a brittle material and any cutting tools used should be sharp, otherwise it is liable to crack. When drilling the holes, start with a small diameter drill, then enlarge it in stages.

Once the Perspex has been cut and drilled, the edges and corners can be smoothed with either a file or glasspaper. A very smooth finish can then be obtained by using metal polish. The base and the two arms should next be degreased using methylated spirits. The base needs to be marked on the reverse side with a screen grid. There is less chance of the grid being rubbed off if it is marked on the reverse side. If desired, the grid could be marked on both sides. A medium-point overhead projection transparency pen can be used to draw this on to the Perspex. These pens can be obtained

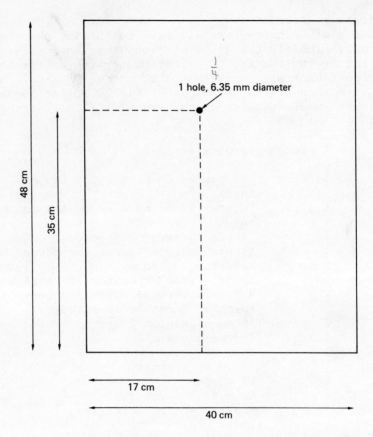

1 hole, 6.35 mm diameter

48 cm

35 cm

17 cm

40 cm

Figure 6.2   Cutting diagram for base of tablet

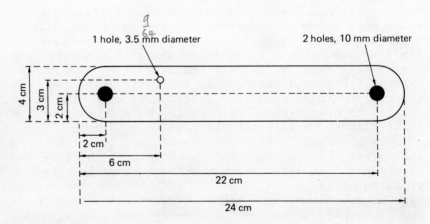

1 hole, 3.5 mm diameter

2 holes, 10 mm diameter

4 cm

3 cm

2 cm

2 cm

6 cm

22 cm

24 cm

Figure 6.3   Cutting diagram for potentiometer arm

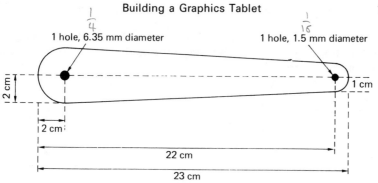

Figure 6.4   Cutting diagram for pointer arm

from good stationers, and come in two sorts:
water-soluble and permanent. The latter sort is better
for this purpose, although mistakes are difficult to
remove. Figure 6.5 shows how the base should be marked
out.

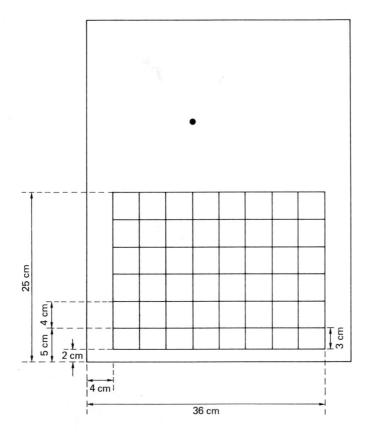

Figure 6.5   Markings for base of tablet

Next the two knobs should be drilled so that the
spindle hole goes all the way through the knob. This
will make the correct positioning of the knobs on the
base and on the pointer arm more precise. Before
gluing, both the arms and the knobs should be free of
grease and dirt. An epoxy resin will provide a strong
bond, and a 6.35 mm bolt can be used to clamp the knobs
on to the Perspex. A small circle of felt should also
be glued on to the other side of the pointer arm,
directly under the knob. This will prevent the arm from
scratching the base of the graphics tablet.

The two potentiometers can then be loosely fastened
on to the potentiometer arm with the terminals facing
each other as in figure 6.6. The potentiometer spindles
will need cutting to length with a small hacksaw. The
potentiometer nearest the small hole for the ´P´ clip
should be fastened to the base of the graphics tablet
and its spindle should be 6 mm longer than the other
spindle. The other potentiometer spindle will need
cutting so that it is just long enough to go through
the knob glued to the pointer arm. It should not
protrude through the arm. Once the spindles have been
cut to the correct length, the potentiometers can be
fastened firmly to the arm.

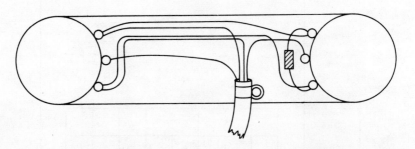

Figure 6.6   Potentiometer arm wiring

At this stage the potentiometer arm and the ´D type´
plug can be wired up. Figures 6.6 and 6.7 show how they
are wired, and figure 6.8 shows the wiring diagram. It
is only as complex as a joystick. The supply voltage is
dropped from 5 volts to 1.75 volts using the 2.7 Kohm
resistor. The resistor is mounted in the plug. The
electrolytic capacitor is wired across the supply lines
to the potentiometers, and can be soldered to the tags
on one of the potentiometers. This capacitor absorbs
minor voltage fluctuations which could cause variations
in the ADVAL readings. Each potentiometer is connected
to the 1.75 volt supply and to the 0 volt supply, and

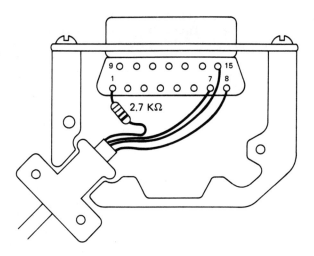

Figure 6.7   ´D type´ plug wiring

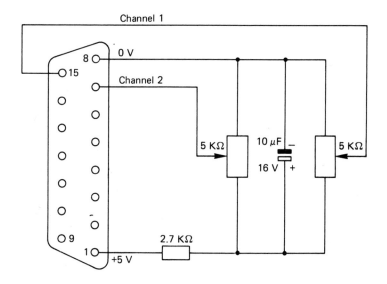

Figure 6.8   Circuit diagram for graphics tablet

the centre tag of each is connected to an analogue input. Once the potentiometers are wired up, the wires can be laced together as shown in figure 6.6, or fastened to the arm with self-adhesive wiring clips. Then the cable can be secured to the arm using the ´P´ clip and the nut and bolt. The two arms are fastened to each other and the base in such a way that both arms point to 12 o´clock when they are rotated fully anticlockwise.

The graphics tablet can be tested using listing 4.1. Channels 1 and 2 should vary when the arms are moved;

channels 3 and 4 will give random readings as they are
unconnected. If just the pointer arm is rotated, then
channel 1 should not change but channel 2 will vary. If
the potentiometer arm is rotated and the pointer arm is
kept still in relation to the potentiometer arm, then
only channel 1 should vary. If the results of these two
operations are reversed, then the connections to pins 7
and 15 of the ´D type´ connector have been reversed.
Next check that the pointer can move over the whole
area of the grid marked on the base. The small hole in
the end of the pointer arm is the actual pointer. Then
using listing 4.1 again, check that the ADVAL readings
remain within range (about 100 to 60000) over the whole
grid area. If the pointer cannot move over the complete
grid area or the ADVAL readings go out of range, then
the appropriate knob needs unscrewing and the arm
altering until the full area remains in range. Once
these checks have been carried out the grub screws in
the knobs should be tightened up until there is no
likelihood of the spindles slipping. A small flat
surface could be filed on the spindle to further reduce
any chance of movement.

The Programs
There are two programs needed for the graphics tablet.
Memory space is at a premium with graphics programs and
this is one way of gaining extra memory. Listing 6.1
calibrates the graphics tablet and defines or loads an
extra character set. Then the second part of the
program, listing 6.2, is loaded in automatically and
this program provides the various drawing routines.
Each program should be typed in and saved on disc or
cassette. If cassette is being used then the second
program must be saved on the same cassette after the
first program. The programs should be saved under the
filenames CH6.1 and CH6.2. If other filenames are used
then the filename at line 80 of listing 6.1 will need
to be changed also. Listing 6.2 is critical on memory,
and the program length should be about 5300 bytes long.
This can be checked, after program entry, by typing

       PRINT TOP-PAGE

and pressing RETURN. If the program length is much
above 5300 bytes long, then first check for extra
spaces that might have been inserted. Often spaces are
inserted at the end of lines where they take up memory
but are otherwise not visible. They can be identified

by changing to mode 6, and typing in the command

VDU23,32,0,126,66,66,66,66,126,0

This line redefines the space as a square, and when the program is listed all the spaces become visible. They can then be removed by recopying the line but not the spaces. If it is desired that extra facilities be included in the program at a later stage, then the space between the line number and the code can be left out. This will free about 300 bytes of memory. More memory can be saved by compacting the lines and using multi-statement lines. Also the lines with the single colons on can be deleted. They have been inserted only to aid clarity.

If the program length is checked after listing 6.2 has been typed in as below and the length is below 5300 bytes, then one or more lines or parts of lines have been missed out. As all the lines are numbered in intervals of 10, missing lines are fairly easy to locate. If this is not found to be the problem, check for missing parts of lines. However, the program length will vary slightly, depending on whether spaces have been inserted or deleted.

```
 10 REM listing 6.1
 20 MODE4
 30 PROCinitialise
 40 PROCset
 50 PROCdefine
 60 CLS
 70 IF PAGE>&E00 THEN PAGE=&1100
 80 CHAIN"CH6.2"
 90 :
100 DEFPROCinitialise
110 *FX4,1
120 *FX225,128
130 C%=1:DIMB 25,C(8)
140 VDU23;8202;0;0;0;
150 VDU19,0,7,0,0,0
160 VDU19,1,4,0,0,0
170 PRINTTAB(12,2)"GRAPHICS TABLET"´
180 ENDPROC
190 :
200 DEFPROCset
210 PRINT"Move pointer to bottom left-hand corner"
220 PRINT"of the grid."
230 PROCspace
240 PROCvalin
250 Ab=A%:Bb=B%
260 PRINT´"Move pointer to top right-hand corner of"
270 PRINT"the grid."
280 PROCspace
290 PROCvalin
```

```
300 At=A%:Bt=B%
310 SF1=1.9963831195/(Ab-At)
320 F%=SF1*1E6
330 SF2=1.0538298/(Bb-Bt)
340 G%=SF2*1E6
350 H%=(1.46607657-Ab*SF1)*1E3
360 I%=(2.18166156-Bb*SF2)*1E3
370 ENDPROC
380 :
390 DEFPROCspace
400 PRINT'"Press space when ready."
410 REPEAT
420 A$=GET$
430 UNTIL A$=" "
440 SOUND1,-15,150,5
450 ENDPROC
460 :
470 DEFPROCvalin
480 A%=0:B%=0
490 FOR N=1 TO 250
500 A%=A%+ADVAL(1)DIV32
510 B%=B%+ADVAL(2)DIV32
520 NEXT N
530 A%=A%/250:B%=B%/250
540 SOUND1,-15,175,5
550 ENDPROC
560 :
570 DEFPROCdefine
580 VDU26,12,18,4,1
590 FOR N=32 TO 416 STEP 48
600 MOVE N,608:DRAW N,992:NEXT N
610 FOR N=608 TO 992 STEP 48
620 MOVE 32,N:DRAW 414,N:NEXT N
630 PRINTTAB(20,0)"SHIFT    CTRL"
640 FOR y=0 TO 9
650 FOR x=0 TO 1
660 PRINTTAB(16,4+y*2)"f";y
670 PRINTTAB(22+x*8,4+y*2)CHR$(128+x*16+y)
680 NEXT x,y
690 x%=32:y%=608
700 PRINTTAB(0,27)"Press function key to be defined,"
710 PRINT"or press L to load definitions,"
720 PRINT"or press S to save definitions"
730 PRINT"or press E to end"
740 A$=GET$
750 IF A$="E" THEN ENDPROC
760 IF A$="S" THEN PROCsave:GOTO580
770 IF A$="L" THEN PROCload:GOTO580
780 C%=ASC(A$)
790 IF C%<128 THEN GOTO740
800 PROCpix
810 REPEAT
820 PROCgetkey
830 UNTIL key=67 OR key=83
840 IFkey=83 THEN GOTO 580
850 VDU23,C%,0,0,0,0,0,0,0,0:GOTO580
860 :
870 DEFPROCsave
```

```
 880 VDU28,0,31,37,27,12
 890 PRINT"Enter file name "
 900 PRINT"max 7 letters ";
 910 INPUTT$
 920 T$=LEFT$(T$,7)
 930 $B="*SAVE "+T$+" C00 CFF"
 940 PROCcli
 950 VDU26
 960 ENDPROC
 970 :
 980 DEFPROCload
 990 VDU28,0,31,37,27,12
1000 PRINT"Enter file name "
1010 PRINT"max 7 letters ";
1020 INPUT T$
1030 T$=LEFT$(T$,7)
1040 $B="*LOAD "+T$
1050 PROCcli
1060 VDU26
1070 ENDPROC
1080 :
1090 DEFPROCgetkey
1100 PRINTTAB(0,26)
1110 PRINT"Use cursor keys to move cross     "
1120 PRINT"Press SPACE to define             "
1130 PRINT"Press S to store definition       "
1140 PRINT"Press C to clear definition       "
1150 VDU5
1160 PROCcross(x%,y%)
1170 key=GET
1180 oldx%=x%:oldy%=y%
1190 IF key=&88 AND x%>32   THEN x%=x%-48
1200 IF key=&89 AND x%<368 THEN x%=x%+48
1210 IF key=&8B AND y%<944 THEN y%=y%+48
1220 IF key=&8A AND y%>608 THEN y%=y%-48
1230 PROCcross(oldx%,oldy%)
1240 VDU4
1250 IFkey=67 OR key=83 THEN ENDPROC
1260 IFkey=&20 THEN PROCsquare:ENDPROC
1270 GOTO1150
1280 :
1290 DEFPROCblock
1300 VDU18,4,129
1310 VDU24,x%+4;y%+4;x%+44;y%+44;
1320 VDU16,26
1330 ENDPROC
1340 :
1350 DEFPROCcross(x%,y%)
1360 VDU18,4,1,25,4,x%+8;y%+36;43
1370 ENDPROC
1380 :
1390 DEFPROCsquare
1400 PROCblock
1410 X%=8-(x%/48)
1420 Y%=(y%/48)-11
1430 IF POINT(x%+8,y%+8)=1 THEN C(Y%)=C(Y%)+2^X%
1440 IF POINT(x%+8,y%+8)=0 THEN C(Y%)=C(Y%)-2^X%
1450 VDU23,C%,C(8),C(7),C(6),C(5),C(4),C(3),C(2),C(1)
```

```
1460 PRINT TAB(22+8*(C%DIV143),4+2*((C%-128)MOD16))
     CHR$C%
1470 ENDPROC
1480 :
1490 DEFPROCpix
1500 X%=0:Y%=13:A%=10:D=&D00
1510 ?D=C%:CALL&FFF1
1520 FOR y=0 TO 7
1530 FOR x=0 TO 7
1540 x%=32+x*48
1550 y%=608+y*48
1560 IF((D?(8-y))AND 2^(7-x))>0 THEN PROCblock
1570 NEXT x,y
1580 FOR N=1 TO 8
1590 C(9-N)=D?N
1600 NEXT N
1610 ENDPROC
1620 :
1630 DEFPROCcli
1640 X%=B MOD256
1650 Y%=B DIV256
1660 CALL&FFF7
1670 ENDPROC
```

Before typing in the next listing, listing 6.1
should be saved on disc or tape.

```
 10 REM listing 6.2
 20 MODE4
 30 PROCborder
 40 PRINTTAB(0,29)"Select mode (0,1,2,4 or 5)";
 50 PROCget1:M%=VAL(A$):MODE M%
 60 PROCinitialise:PROCgetkey
 70 REPEAT:x%=X%:y%=Y%
 80 PROCcursor(x%,y%):PROCadval
 90 PROCget2:PROCcursor(x%,y%)
100 IFA$<>"":CLS:PROCgetkey
110 UNTIL 0
120 :
130 DEFPROCinitialise
140 *FX16,2
150 *FX11,0
160 DIM F 75,f(1,1),Q%(75),P% 40,A 10
170 f%=P%+20:@%=0
180 [:OPT0:.f6%:LDX#f% MOD256:LDY#f% DIV256
190 LDA#&D:JSR&FFF1:RTS:]
200 VDU23;8202;0;0;0;
210 N%=2^(1+M% MOD 3):n%=N%-1
220 IF M%>3 THEN n%=(N%/2)-1
230 CLS:C%=n%
240 VDU28,0,31,(160/N%)-1,29
250 PROCborder
260 ENDPROC
270 :
280 DEFPROCgetkey
290 IF A$="D" THEN PROCdefine
```

```
300 IF A$="A" THEN PROCalter
310 IF A$="S" THEN PROCsave
320 IF A$="X" THEN PROCload
330 IF A$="W" THEN PROCwipe
340 IF A$="L" THEN PROCline
350 IF A$="R" THEN PROCrectangle
360 IF A$="C" THEN PROCcircle
370 IF A$="I" THEN PROCinfill
380 IF A$="P" THEN PROCprint
390 IF A$="F" THEN PROCfollow
400 COLOUR n%:CLS
410 PRINT"Command?"
420 GCOL0,C%:PROCborder
430 ENDPROC
440 :
450 DEFPROCdefine
460 FOR T=0 TO n%
470 INPUT"Enter colour number"´"(0-15) "C
480 VDU19,T,C,0,0,0
490 NEXT T
500 ENDPROC
510 :
520 DEFPROCalter
530 PROCcolour
540 INPUT´"Which colour now "C%
550 ENDPROC
560 :
570 DEFPROCsave
580 PROCnamefile
590 IF M%>3 THEN N$=" 5800 " ELSE N$=" 3000 "
600 $A="SAVE "+T$+N$+"7FFF"+CHR$(13)
610 PROCcli
620 ENDPROC
630 :
640 DEFPROCload
650 PROCnamefile
660 $A="LOAD "+T$+CHR$(13)
670 PROCcli
680 ENDPROC
690 :
700 DEFPROCcli
710 X%=A MOD 256:Y%=A DIV 256
720 CALL&FFF7
730 ENDPROC
740 :
750 DEFPROCwipe
760 PRINT"OK to clear screen?"
770 PROCget1:IF A$="Y" THEN CLG
780 ENDPROC
790 :
800 DEFPROCline
810 PRINT"Sloping, Horizontal or Vertical line?";
820 PROCget1:L%=INSTR("HV",A$)
830 PROClinetype:PROCsp
840 REPEAT:PROCadval
850 IF L%=1 THEN Y%=y%
860 IF L%=2 THEN X%=x%
870 PROCli(6+D%):PROCget2:PROCli(6+D%)
```

```
 880 UNTIL A$=" "
 890 PROCli(5+D%)
 900 ENDPROC
 910 :
 920 DEFPROCrectangle
 930 PROClinetype:PROCsp
 940 REPEAT:PROCadval
 950 PROCre(6+D%):PROCget2:PROCre(6+D%)
 960 UNTIL A$=" "
 970 PROCre(5+D%)
 980 ENDPROC
 990 :
1000 DEFPROCcircle
1010 INPUT"Number of sides "P%
1020 PROClinetype:PROCsp
1030 PROCcursor(x%,y%)
1040 REPEAT
1050 PROCadval:PROCcursor(X%,Y%):PROCci(6+D%)
1060 PROCget2:PROCci(6+D%):PROCcursor(X%,Y%)
1070 UNTIL A$=" "
1080 PROCcursor(x%,y%):PLOT69,x%,y%:PROCci(5+D%)
1090 ENDPROC
1100 :
1110 DEFPROCinfill
1120 f(0,0)=n%:f(0,1)=n%:f(1,1)=n%:f(1,0)=n%
1130 IF N%>2 THEN PROCpixeldef
1140 REPEAT:y%=y%+4:UNTIL POINT(x%,y%)<>0
1150 y%=y%-8:Yl%=y%:Xl%=x%
1160 PROCfi:y%=Yl%:x%=Xl%
1170 ENDPROC
1180 :
1190 DEFPROCprint
1200 PRINT"Double height Y/N":PROCgetl
1210 IFA$="Y" THEN ps=2 ELSE ps=1
1220 PRINT"Horizontal or vertical H/V":PROCgetl
1230 INPUTLINE"Enter print"'P$
1240 V$=CHR$10+CHR$8
1250 IF ps=2 THEN V$=CHR$10+V$
1260 IF A$="V" THEN v$="":FOR ve=1 TO LENP$:
     v$=v$+MID$(P$,ve,1)+V$:NEXT ve:P$=v$
1270 PROCsp:REPEAT:PROCadval:x%=X%:y%=Y%
1280 PROCpr(4,ps):PROCget2:PROCpr(4,ps)
1290 UNTIL A$=" "
1300 PROCpr(0,ps)
1310 ENDPROC
1320 :
1330 DEFPROCfollow
1340 PRINT"Follow mode":PROCsp
1350 REPEAT:PROCadval:PROCget2
1360 DRAW X%,Y%:UNTIL A$=" "
1370 ENDPROC
1380 :
1390 DEFPROCli(K)
1400 MOVEx%,y%:PLOTK,X%,Y%
1410 ENDPROC
1420 :
1430 DEFPROCre(K)
1440 MOVEx%,y%:PLOTK,X%,y%
```

```
1450 PLOTK,X%,Y%:PLOTK,x%,Y%
1460 PLOTK,x%,y%
1470 ENDPROC
1480 :
1490 DEFPROCci(K)
1500 cs=2*PI/P%
1510 cr=SQR((Y%-y%)^2+(X%-x%)^2)
1520 IF cr<2*N% THEN ENDPROC
1530 ca=ATN((X%-x%)/(0.5+Y%-y%))
1540 IF Y%<y% THEN ca=ca+PI:ELSE IF X%<x% THEN
     ca=ca+2*PI
1550 MOVE X%,Y%
1560 FOR cn=1 TO P%
1570 PLOTK,x%+cr*SIN(ca+cn*cs),y%+cr*COS(ca+cn*cs)
1580 NEXT cn
1590 ENDPROC
1600 :
1610 DEFPROCpr(pc,d)
1620 VDU5,18,pc,C%,25,4,x%;y%+32*d;
1630 IFd=1:PRINTP$:VDU4:ENDPROC
1640 A%=10:X%=0:Y%=10:p=&A00
1650 FOR pb%=1 TO LEN(P$)
1660 p$=MID$(P$,pb%,1)
1670 IF p$<" " THEN PRINTp$;:GOTO1720
1680 ?p=ASC(p$):CALL&FFF1
1690 VDU23,240,p?1,p?1,p?2,p?2,p?3,p?3,p?4,p?4
1700 VDU23,241,p?5,p?5,p?6,p?6,p?7,p?7,p?8,p?8
1710 VDU240,8,10,241,11;
1720 NEXT pb%
1730 VDU4
1740 ENDPROC
1750 :
1760 DEFPROCadval
1770 V1%=0:V2%=0
1780 FOR n=1 TO 25
1790 V1%=V1%+ADVAL(1)DIV32
1800 V2%=V2%+ADVAL(2)DIV32
1810 NEXT n
1820 t1=V1%*F%*4E-8+H%*1E-3
1830 t3=V2%*G%*4E-8+I%*1E-3
1840 t2=t3-t1
1850 X%=N%*((520+800*(COSt1-COSt2))DIVN%)
1860 Y%=4*((1416-800*(SINt1+SINt2))DIV4)
1870 IFY%<96Y%=96:ELSEIFY%>1023Y%=1023
1880 IFX%<0:X%=0ELSEIFX%>1279:X%=1279
1890 PRINTTAB(0,2)"X="X%;" Y="Y%;"    ";
1900 ENDPROC
1910 :
1920 DEFPROClinetype
1930 D%=0
1940 PRINT"Solid or dotted S/D";
1950 PROCget1:IFA$="D" THEN D%=16
1960 ENDPROC
1970 :
1980 DEFPROCcursor(x,y)
1990 MOVE x-16,y:PLOT 6,x+16,y
2000 MOVE x,y-16:PLOT 6,x,y+16
2010 ENDPROC
```

```
2020 :
2030 DEFPROCget1
2040 A$=GET$:PROCkeyconvert:CLS
2050 ENDPROC
2060 :
2070 DEFPROCnamefile
2080 S%=1:IF PAGE=&E00:S%=0
2090 IF S%=0 THEN *OPT1,1
2100 IF S%=0 THEN *OPT2,1
2110 INPUT"Enter title "T$
2120 T$=LEFT$(T$,7)
2130 ENDPROC
2140 :
2150 DEFPROCget2
2160 A$=INKEY$(2):PROCkeyconvert
2170 ENDPROC
2180 :
2190 DEFPROCkeyconvert
2200 a=ASCA$:IF a>13 THEN SOUND1,-15,150,5
2210 IF a>96 AND a<123 THEN A$=CHR$(a-32)
2220 IF a>32 AND a<48 THEN A$=CHR$(a+16)
2230 ENDPROC
2240 :
2250 DEFPROCpixeldef
2260 FOR n=0 TO 1
2270 FOR N=0 TO 1
2280 PROCfillcolours
2290 PRINTTAB(3,2)"Colour for "CHR$(65+N+2*n);
2300 REPEAT
2310 PROCget1
2320 f(N,n)=VALA$
2330 UNTIL f(N,n)>0 AND f(N,n) <n%+1
2340 NEXT N,n
2350 PROCfillcolours
2360 ENDPROC
2370 :
2380 DEFPROCborder
2390 MOVE 0,96:DRAW 1279,96
2400 DRAW 1279,1023:DRAW 0,1023
2410 DRAW0,96
2420 ENDPROC
2430 :
2440 DEFPROCfillcolours
2450 FOR n1=0 TO 1
2460 FOR n2=0 TO 1
2470 COLOURf(n2,n1)
2480 F$=CHR$(65+n2+2*n1)
2490 PRINTTAB(n2,n1)F$
2500 NEXT n2,n1
2510 PROCcolour
2520 ENDPROC
2530 :
2540 DEFPROCsp
2550 PRINT"Press space to end"
2560 ENDPROC
2570 :
2580 DEFPROCcolour
2590 PRINTTAB(3,0)"Colours";
```

```
2600 FOR T=0 TO n%
2610 COLOUR T:PRINT T;:NEXT T
2620 ENDPROC
2630 :
2640 DEFPROCfi
2650 fl%=1:f2%=0
2660 PROCfa(x%)
2670 REPEAT
2680 f3%=Q%(fl%):f4%=Q%(fl%+25)
2690 y%=4+Q%(fl%+50):fl%=(fl%+1)MOD25
2700 PROCfc
2710 y%=y%-8
2720 PROCfc
2730 UNTILfl%=f2%+1
2740 ENDPROC
2750 :
2760 DEFPROCfc
2770 IF POINT(f3%,y%)<1 THEN f8%=f3%:ELSE PROCfb(f3%)
2780 IFf8% > f4%-N% THEN ENDPROC
2790 REPEAT
2800 PROCfa(f8%)
2810 PROCfb(f8%)
2820 UNTILf8%>f4%
2830 ENDPROC
2840 :
2850 DEFPROCfa(x%)
2860 PLOT76,x%,y%
2870 CALLf6%
2880 f2%=(f2%+1)MOD25
2890 Q%(f2%)=!f%AND&FFFF
2900 Q%(f2%+25)=f%!4AND&FFFF
2910 PROCfd(Q%(f2%),Q%(f2%+25))
2920 Q%(f2%+50)=y%
2930 ENDPROC
2940 :
2950 DEFPROCfb(f10%)
2960 PLOT92,f10%,y%:CALLf6%
2970 f8%=N%+f%!4 AND &FFFF
2980 IF f8%>f4% THEN f5%=f4% ELSE f5%=f8%-N%
2990 PROCfd(f10%,f5%)
3000 ENDPROC
3010 :
3020 DEFPROCfd(f10%,f11%)
3030 IF POINT(f11%,y%)<>0 THEN ENDPROC
3040 Y%=(y%DIV4)MOD2
3050 X%=(f10%DIVN%)MOD2
3060 GCOL0,f(X%,Y%):PLOT77,f11%,y%
3070 GCOL0,f((X%+1)MOD2,Y%)
3080 MOVEf10%+N%,y%:PLOT21,f11%,y%
3090 ENDPROC
3100 :
3110 DEFPROCdump
3120 ENDPROC
```

DESCRIPTION OF LISTING 6.1

The descriptions of these programs are short as they are all in procedure form, and the function of each procedure is not too difficult to work out. Listing 6.1 calls up three main procedures: PROCinitialise, PROCset and PROCdefine. It next clears the screen, moves PAGE down to &1100 if a disc or Econet machine is being used, and then CHAINs the next program, CH6.2. PROCinitialise sets the screen display and initialises any variables needed by the program.

PROCset is the procedure to calibrate the tablet. It reads the positions of the pointer at the bottom-left-hand and top-right-hand corners of the screen and calculates three scaling factors which are stored in G%, H% and I%. The values in these integer variables are not lost when the second program loads in. PROCvalin is the procedure to read the Analogue Port. For greater accuracy, the Analogue Port is read 250 times and the results are averaged.

PROCdefine is the procedure to define the 20 user-defined characters. A grid is drawn on the screen and characters defined are printed on the screen. When a new character is selected, its pixel pattern if already defined is inserted in the grid and so existing definitions can be altered. PROCdefine calls up several other procedures. PROCload and PROCsave load and save the definitions. PROCgetkey is used to move the cursor around the grid and to set or clear a pixel. PROCcross draws a cross to indicate the cursor position. PROCblock fills in a pixel when set. PROCsquare reads the pixels set on the grid, defines the character, and prints the character in the correct position on the screen. PROCpix looks at the memory area where the definitions are stored to find the dot pattern of the character. This is then printed in the grid when that particular character is selected for definition. PROCcli is a short procedure to access the command line interpreter. It is needed by PROCload and PROCsave to load and save the character set with the user's own filename.

DESCRIPTION OF LISTING 6.2

This program is loaded when the first program has finished. Once the mode has been selected the screen clears and single key presses will select each of the various routines outlined at the start of the chapter. PROCgetkey routes the program to a separate set of drawing routines, depending on the key pressed. Many of the drawing routines work by first drawing the shape, then inverting the colour and redrawing the same shape.

This effectively 'undraws' the shape. Hence the shape can be moved about the screen. When the space bar is pressed the shape is again drawn but this time it is not 'undrawn' and the routine ends.

USING THE GRAPHICS TABLET
The graphics tablet is first plugged into the Analogue Port at the back of the BBC computer. Then the first program, listing 6.1, is loaded in. When this program has loaded in, the pointer should be positioned at the bottom-left-hand corner of the grid. Once the pointer has been positioned the space bar is pressed. The computer will bleep. The pointer must not be moved until the computer bleeps again. Then the pointer should be moved to the top-right-hand corner of the grid. Once the pointer has been positioned, the space bar should be pressed again. The computer will again bleep to signal that it has registered the pressing of the space bar. Again the pointer must not be moved until the computer beeps again. This then completes the calibration of the graphics tablet.

There are many occasions when it would be useful to define small characters that are too small to be drawn directly. The characters can be defined once the tablet has been calibrated, and this allows the user to incorporate up to 20 different user-defined characters. The 20 characters are accessed using the red function keys and the SHIFT or CTRL key. Once the definer has appeared on the screen there is the option of loading in a new set of characters, saving an existing character set, defining a character, or ending the definer. If the user just wants to use an existing set of characters, then this set should be loaded in and 'E' pressed to exit from the generator.

When loading or saving a character set, the filename must have seven or fewer letters. The program truncates longer filenames to seven letters. A new character can be defined by pressing the SHIFT or CTRL key together with the function key to be defined. Any character already defined for that key will be drawn in the grid, so existing characters can be altered. The cross can be moved using the cursor arrows, and the pixel set or cleared using the space bar. The character will be drawn in the appropriate position in the table on the right. When satisfied with the character, you can save it by pressing 'S'. The character can be cleared completely by pressing 'C'. When all the characters have been defined they should be saved to disc or tape. Once saved, pressing 'E' will load the second program, listing 6.2.

Once listing 6.2 has loaded, the screen will clear

and the user will be invited to select a BBC graphics
mode. All the drawing modes available on the BBC can be
used. Modes 3, 6 and 7 are not drawing modes and should
not be used. Once a mode has been selected, the screen
will be ready for a command.

To use any command, the pointer is first positioned
at the required start position, then the desired key is
pressed. Instructions will appear in the window at the
bottom of the screen. A screen cursor, a small flashing
cross, will indicate the current pointer position. This
screen cursor will disappear when any command key is
pressed and will reappear only when the command has
been finished. A bleep will sound to indicate that a
key has been pressed. Apart from the BREAK and ESCAPE
keys, pressing a key not used for a command will have
no effect.

When the computer is waiting for a command the word
´Command?´ will show in the window at the bottom of the
screen. The program will accept commands which are
typed in with the CAPS LOCK or SHIFT LOCK buttons
either on or off and normally the RETURN key is not
needed.

R ... Draw a rectangle
The pointer is positioned at one corner of the
rectangle to be drawn and ´R´ is pressed. As the
pointer is moved, a flashing rectangle will be
displayed on the screen; the size of the rectangle can
be changed by moving the pointer. To ´fix´ the
rectangle, the space bar has to be pressed. The
rectangle will stop flashing and appear in the current
drawing colour. A rectangle can be drawn also with
dotted lines.

L ... Draw a line
The pointer is moved to one end of the line to be drawn
and ´L´ is pressed. Either a horizontal line, a
vertical line, or a sloping line can be selected. The
option is selected by pressing either ´H´, ´V´ or ´S´.
The line can be solid or dotted. As the pointer is
moved, a flashing line will appear. As before, the line
can be ´fixed´ by pressing the space bar.

C ... Draw a circle or polygon
Move the pointer to the centre of the circle to be
drawn and press ´C´. The user is then asked for the
number of sides. This enables regular polygons to be
drawn. Any number above 3 can be entered. A number
above about 30 will effectively draw a circle. Entering
a number above 50 will slow the routine down
considerably. The centre of the polygon will be at the

pointer position when ´C´ was pressed. The polygon will
draw and undraw as the pointer is moved, and one corner
of the polygon will be where the pointer directs. Hence
it is possible to alter the size of the polygon and to
rotate it to the desired position about its centre.

F ... Follow mode

This mode is useful for drawing irregular shapes such
as outlines of maps. The pointer is positioned at the
start of the shape to be drawn and F is pressed. Now a
line will be drawn on the screen as the pointer is
moved. Follow mode can be stopped by pressing the space
bar.

P ... Print at

Text can be entered in the window at the bottom of the
screen when ´P´ is pressed. Double-height or single-
height text can be selected, as can horizontal or
vertical text. The text will be printed on the drawing
area as a flashing image when RETURN is pressed, and
can be moved to the correct position by the pointer. It
is ´fixed´ in the usual way by pressing the space bar,
when it will be printed in the correct position. The
user-defined characters can be included in the print
statements by pressing combinations of the SHIFT or
CTRL key and the function keys.

D ... Define colours

This command is not easy to understand because of the
complexity of the BBC microcomputer´s colour options
and the wish to make all the options available to the
user. The commands closely follow the BBC´s actual
colour commands (the COLOUR, GCOL and VDU19 commands).
The graphics tablet can therefore be used to
demonstrate or gain more understanding of the
relationships between logical and actual colours. It is
suggested that the user also refers to the User Guide
reference sections on colour and mode.

The colours available to the user depend on the mode
chosen. As can be seen from the following table the
more colours required the poorer becomes the horizontal
resolution. It is left to the user to decide which is
the best compromise.

BBC Mode	Colours Avail.	Horiz. Res.	Vert. Res.	Memory Used
0	2	640	256	20K
1	4	320	256	20K
2	8	160	256	20K
4	2	320	256	10K
5	4	160	256	10K

The actual colours are numbered as follows

```
colour 0 ... black
colour 1 ... red
colour 2 ... green
colour 3 ... yellow
colour 4 ... blue
colour 5 ... magenta
colour 6 ... cyan
colour 7 ... white
colour 8 ... flashing black/white
colour 9 ... flashing red/cyan
colour 10... flashing green/magenta
colour 11... flashing yellow/blue
colour 12... flashing blue/yellow
colour 13... flashing magenta/green
colour 14... flashing cyan/red
colour 15... flashing white/black
```

Any of the logical colours can be changed using the 'D' key. The computer asks which colour it is to be changed to. The reply will be a number from 0 to 15 from the list of actual colours given above. The colours cannot be changed during another command.

A ... Alter colour

This command allows the user to select a new drawing colour. On pressing the 'A' key a series of numbers will appear in different colours. In modes 0 and 4 the number 1 only will be printed as these modes are two-colour modes. In modes 1 and 5 the numbers 1, 2 and 3 will appear in the colours defined. The new colour selected is shown by the colour of the border round the picture-drawing area. Should the line disappear then the colour chosen is the same as the background colour. After pressing 'A' the user is asked 'Which colour now' and a number must be entered. This number can be either 0 or 1 if in modes 0 and 4, from 0 to 3 if in modes 1 or 5 or from 0 to 7 if in mode 2. The number referred to represents the logical colour and not the actual colour. The colour must be changed before another command is used.

W ... Wipes the screen clear

Pressing 'W' will clear the screen. The computer will respond with 'OK to clear screen?'. If 'Y' is typed in then the picture will be erased.

S ... Saves the picture

Once 'S' has been pressed the user is asked for a title. If a tape is being used, the instruction 'RECORD THEN RETURN' will appear. This enables the user to position the tape at the desired point. If a tape recorder with motor control is being used, the user will now be able to wind or rewind the tape. Press PLAY and RECORD together on the tape and then press RETURN. Now the computer will save the picture. If using disc, the picture will save once the filename has been entered. A picture can be saved at any time and it is worth while saving parts of a picture as it is being developed.

I ... Infill a shape with colour

Move the pointer inside the shape to be filled in. The pointer must be inside the shape and the shape must be closed, otherwise the colour will 'leak' out. When using a drawing mode that offers 4 or 8 colours, a textured fill routine is available. This greatly extends the range of infilling colours available. It works by the user defining a 'super pixel', that is, a block of 4 ordinary pixels. Any available colour except the background colour can be put in any of the 4 small pixels that make up the super pixel. The user is advised to experiment with this feature first to explore the range of new colours and textures that can be produced.

Do not try to infill a shape drawn using dotted lines as the infilling will leak out. The infill routine will infill only from the background colour. It will not work over a previously filled area.

X ... Print picture out

This facility has been included in 'skeleton' form to allow the picture to be dumped on to a printer. Routines for Acorn, Seikosha and Epson printers have been included here. They are written in BASIC and are quite short, yet enable a picture to be printed out speedily. They can also be adapted to suit other printers. It is also possible to call up print dump-routines resident in ROMs. The print-dump routine can be added at the end of the second program (listing 6.2) in the procedure, starting at line 3110. Listing 6.2 will need to be saved with the printer routine included.

a. Acorn/Seikosha GP80/GP100 printers

```
3110 DEFPROCDUMP:VDU2,1,8
3120 FOR Y%=1023 TO 83 STEP-28
3130 FOR X%=0 TO 1277 STEP3:D%=0
3140 FOR y%=27 TO 0 STEP-4:D%=D%*2
3150 IF POINT(X%,Y%-y%)>0 THEN D%=D%+1
3160 NEXT y%:VDU1,D%+128:NEXT X%
3170 VDU1,10:NEXT Y%:VDU1,15,3
3180 ENDPROC
```

b. Epson MX80,RX80,FX80 printers

```
3110 DEFPROCDUMP:VDU2,1,27,1,51,1,24
3120 FOR Y% = 1023 TO 95 STEP-16
3130 VDU2,1,27,1,75,1,170,1,1
3140 FOR X% = 0 TO 1277 STEP3:D%=0
3150 FOR y%=0 TO 7:D%=D%*2
3160 IF POINT(X%,Y%-y%*2)>0 THEN D%=D%+1
3170 NEXT y%:VDU1,D%:NEXT X%
3180 VDU1,10:NEXT Y%:VDU3:ENDPROC
```

Note that for both of these routines, if the printer does not have line feed set, change the ´VDU1,10:´ command to read ´VDU1,10,1,13:´.

Z ... Load picture
This command allows a picture to be loaded in from tape (or disc). A picture can be started and saved, and later re-entered to be finished.

Using the pictures within programs
Once drawn and saved, pictures can be called up from programs by inserting the line

        *LOAD"picture"

in the program, where ´picture´ is the filename under which the picture was saved. The colours will not necessarily be the same and so they will need to be changed using the VDU19 statement.

7 Using the BBC Machine as a Multimeter

This project uses simple cheap components to make a voltmeter and ammeter that will display the readings on the microcomputer screen. There are two programs: the first displays the reading as an analogue meter; the second displays the result as a digital meter. Both programs have automatic scaling. The program changes the range of readings without the user having to set switches. The analogue-display program allows the user to select the full-scale deflection of the meter display to be x2, x5 or x10. A switch is fitted on the multimeter to allow this function. There are 3 switches on the meter (see figure 7.1). The second switch is the current/voltage selection switch, and the third switch is a range switch to extend the range of readings by 10. One feature of the multimeter is that once the program is running, there is no keyboard input needed at all.

The multimeter is constructed in a plastic box with an aluminium lid. These boxes can be obtained from most electronics shops and by mail order. They make construction easy and improve the presentation of the finished project. The multimeter uses one analogue channel to sense the input voltage and the other three channels to sense the positions of the range switch, the scale switch and the volts/amps switch. This means that the program can be controlled from the multimeter without the need for any keyboard input into the computer. The type of measurement and multiplier is printed at the bottom of the screen in double-height lettering.

The multimeter will read voltages in the range millivolts to 18 volts. The ammeter will read current in the range milliamps to 5 amps. There is a x1 and x0.1 range switch on the meter. This should normally be set to x0.1, so that the maximum voltages and currents can be read, and switched to x1 only for small voltages and currents. The multimeter is internally protected so that voltages above 1.8 volts do not destroy the digital-to-analogue converter. However, this internal protection is proof only against voltages up to about 75 volts. This multimeter **must never** be used to measure the mains voltage, and it is unwise to connect it to a supply greater than 30 volts. Apart from the risk of doing permanent damage to the computer, there is a danger of suffering an electric shock.

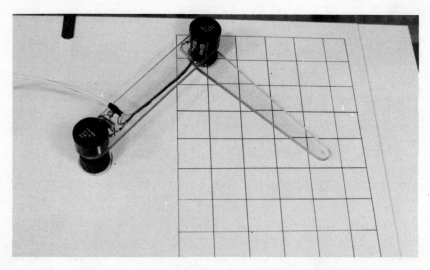

Figure 7.1   Photograph of multimeter

Materials required

1	15 pin ´D type´ connector
1	15 pin ´D type´ connector cover
1 m	6-core cable
1	Plastic box with aluminium lid at least 65 mm x 120 mm x 40 mm deep.
1	Terminal, red
1	Terminal, black
1	3-pole, 4-way rotary switch
2	Double-pole double-throw miniature toggle switch. DC current rating 5 amps
1	1 ohm wirewound resistor, 5 watt
1	8.2 Kohm resister, 0.25 watt
1	1.0 Kohm resister, 0.25 watt
1	27 Kohm resister, 0.25 watt
1	47 Kohm resister, 0.25 watt
5	1N914 diodes, or equivalent

Construction

There are a number of ways in which this project can be constructed and, as the circuit is simple, no set

construction method will be given here. It can be
constructed on Veroboard, which can then be fastened
inside the box, or the components can be wired directly
to the switches. There are plenty of spare solder tags
on the wafer switch, and these can be used for the
diode chain. The aluminium front panel can be labelled
with rub-down lettering, and then covered with a piece
of clear book-covering film. A suggested front panel
layout is shown in figure 7.2. The circuit can be
separated into two parts: the actual multimeter circuit
(figure 7.3), and the switch positions feedback
circuits (figure 7.4).

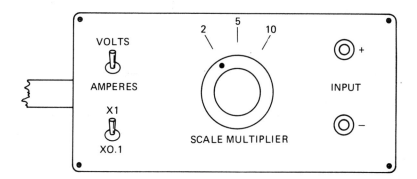

Figure 7.2   Front panel layout

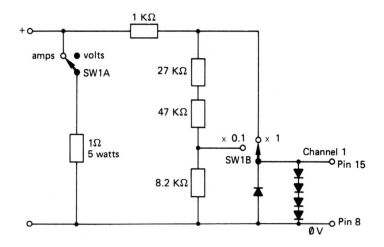

Figure 7.3 Circuit diagram of multimeter

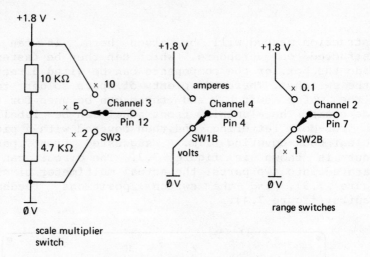

Figure 7.4 Feedback circuits

None of the components is difficult to obtain. The five diodes are in the circuit as a form of input protection: one is to prevent reverse voltages, the other four are to prevent overvoltage conditions. As diodes do not start conducting until the voltage across them is 0.5 volts, the diode chain will not start to conduct until the voltage rises to about 2 volts. The 1 Kohm resistor in series with the input limits the current that would flow through the diodes, but otherwise plays an insignificant part in the circuit. These diodes will stand a maximum current of 75 mA. The diodes have a black band at the cathode end. It is this end which should be wired towards the 0 volt line.

The x0.1 range is achieved by using a voltage divider. This is the 27 Kohm, the 47 Kohm and the 8.2 Kohm resistor network. The 27 Kohm resistor and the 47 Kohm resistor can be replaced by a single 74 Kohm resistor if one is obtainable.

The miniature toggle switch to be used for the amps/volts switch needs to have a direct current rating of 5 amps. Lower-rated switches can be used but then the maximum current that can be input must similarly be reduced. The current rating of the wafer switch and the other toggle switch is unimportant as these switch low currents only.

TESTING THE MULTIMETER
Once the multimeter has been constructed, it can be tested using listing 4.1. This avoids the problem, should difficulties arise, of having to decide if the meter is faulty or whether there is a mistake in the program. (Hopefully there will be neither!) Channel 2

should give a low reading (less then 256) when the
range switch is set to x1. It should go high (over
60000, or a blank display) when the switch is set to
x0.1. Channel 3 is the range switch. With the switch
set to the x2 position, there should be a low reading;
with the switch set to the x5 position a value just
over 20000 should register; and when changed to x10
there should be a high value.

Channel 1 should give a low reading when
disconnected, but when a 1.5 volt dry battery is
connected across the terminals then the reading should
rise to about 50000.

THE ANALOGUE DISPLAY PROGRAM

This program simulates the display of a traditional
analogue meter. This program can create thirty
different scales. The full-scale deflection can be
selected by a switch on the meter to be either 2, 5 or
10. The meter is autoranging, that is to say the
computer will choose the best decade range to use and
will display the correct units and multiplier. It reads
from 0.001 to 99.99 in decade ranges. It is possible to
go out of range when the x2 or x5 scale setting is
being used. If this happens, the pointer will stop just
off the end of the scale.

The program is quite complicated, mainly because of
the screen display; the actual part of the program that
inputs information from the Analogue Port is short.
There are five procedures in listing 7.1. The first
procedure PROCinitialise sets all the start variables
to their correct values, switches off the cursor, and
redefines the colours.

PROCscale draws the scale on the screen. It first
puts the appropriate number of double-height figures on
the screen and then draws the scale itself. The scale
changes in accordance with the full-scale deflection
required, that is 0-2, 0-5 or 0-10. Markers are placed
on the screen to subdivide each interval. This
complicates the procedure, because of the different
length markers required in different positions.

PROCbezel draws the yellow bezel at the bottom of
the screen. The units and the multiplying factor are
printed in the middle of the bezel in blue. PROCpointer
first checks the Analogue Port and then draws the
previous pointer in the background colour to erase it
before drawing the new pointer position in red.

PROCdouble is the double-height print routine used
throughout the book. PROCadval reads channel 1 of the
Analogue Port 100 times. (It should be pointed out that
the ADVAL reading will not be updated as fast as the

loop will repeat. Therefore, there will be far fewer than 100 ADVAL readings summed. The alternative is to force an ADVAL conversion each time, and sum a smaller number of readings.) It then reads the other three channels to sense the switch positions. Channel 2 is the range multiplier switch. If the switch is set to x1 then the ADVAL reading will be 0; if set to the x0.1 range then the ADVAL reading will be greater than 0. R% stores a 0 if the range switch is set to 0 and a 1 if the range switch is set to x0.1. Channel 3 senses the scale switch. This is stored in the variable S%, a value of 0 representing a full-scale deflection of 2, a value of 1 representing a full-scale deflection of 5 and a value of 2 represents a full-scale deflection of 10. Channel 4 senses the volts/amps switch, and returns a value of 0 in I% for the volts range and a value of 1 in I% for the amps range.

The actual meter-reading value is stored in the variable V. The value of V is tested to check the multiplier factor. Once the multiplier has been determined the value of V is reduced to keep it in the range 1-10. Lastly the scale and bezel are checked to see if they have changed. If they have, then that part of the screen is updated by the appropriate procedure. This is better than redrawing the whole of the screen. It takes less time and gives some continuity to the display.

```
 10 REM listing 7.1
 20 MODE1
 30 PROCinitialise
 40 REPEAT
 50 PROCpointer
 60 UNTIL 0
 70 :
 80 DEFPROCinitialise
 90 @%=0:T%=2:V=0
100 bezel$="":scale=0
110 VDU19,0,7,0,0,0
120 VDU19,3,0,0,0,0
130 VDU23;8202;0;0;0;
140 PX=596:PY=253:angle=1.4
150 ENDPROC
160 :
170 DEFPROCscale
180 X1=156:Y1=693
190 GCOL0,128
200 CLG
210 GCOL0,3
220 FOR S=0 TO fsd STEP 1
230 angle=1.4*S/fsd+0.869
240 X=ABS(-624+(850*COS(angle)))
250 Y=120+850*SIN(angle)
260 PROCdouble(STR$(S),X,Y)
```

```
270 NEXT S
280 FOR S=0 TO 20
290 angle=(1.4*S/20)+0.869:L=740
300 IF fsd=2:IF S MOD5=0 THEN L=L-24:IF S MOD10=0
    THEN L=L-24
310 IF fsd>2:IF S MOD2=0 THEN L=L-24
315 IF fsd=5 AND S MOD4=0 THEN L=L-24
320 X=ABS(-640+(L*COS(angle)))
330 Y=120+L*SIN(angle)
340 MOVE X,Y
350 X=ABS(-640+(764*COS(angle)))
360 Y=120+764*SIN(angle)
370 DRAW X,Y
380 DRAW X1,Y1
390 X1=X:Y1=Y
400 NEXT S
410 ENDPROC
420 :
430 DEFPROCbezel
440 GCOL0,130
450 VDU24,0;0;1279;250;
460 CLG
470 GCOL0,3
480 X=640-(32*LEN(U$))
490 PROCdouble(U$,X,175)
500 VDU24,0;250;1279;1023;
510 ENDPROC
520 :
530 DEFPROCpointer
540 OPX=PX:OPY=PY:OV=V:OA=angle
550 PROCadval
560 GCOL0,0
570 MOVE(640-(200/TAN(OA))),253
580 DRAW OPX,OPY
590 V=V*1.4/(fsd*10)
600 IF V>1.45 THEN V=1.45
610 GCOL0,1
620 angle=0.869+V
630 PY=50+750*SIN(angle)
640 PX=ABS(-640+680*COS(angle))
650 MOVE(640-(200/TAN(angle))),253
660 DRAW PX,PY
670 ENDPROC
680 :
690 DEFPROCdouble(A$,K,L)
700 LOCAL N
710 VDU5
720 A%=&A:X%=0:Y%=&A:D=&A00
730 FOR N=1 TO LEN(A$)
740 K1=K+(64*(N-1))
750 B$=MID$(A$,N,1)
760 ?D=ASC(B$)
770 CALL &FFF1
780 VDU23,240,D?1,D?1,D?2,D?2,D?3,D?3,D?4,D?4
790 VDU23,241,D?5,D?5,D?6,D?6,D?7,D?7,D?8,D?8
800 MOVE K1,L:PRINTCHR$(240);
810 MOVE K1,L-32:PRINTCHR$(241);
820 NEXT N
```

```
 830 VDU4
 840 ENDPROC
 850 :
 860 DEFPROCadval
 870 V=0
 880 FOR N=1 TO 100
 890 V=V+ADVAL(1)/32
 900 NEXT N
 910 V=V*18/2048
 920 I%=ADVAL(4) DIV32000
 930 S%=ADVAL(3) DIV20000
 940 R%=ADVAL(2) DIV32000
 950 IF R%>0 THEN V=V*10
 960 IF I%>0 THEN U$="AMPERES" ELSE U$="VOLTS"
 970 IF S%>1 THEN fsd=10
 980 IF S%=1 THEN fsd=5
 990 IF S%=0 THEN fsd=2
1000 IF V<1000 THEN U$="MILLI"+U$
1010 IF V>9 AND V<100 THEN U$=U$+" x 10":T%=1
1020 IF V>99 AND V<1000 THEN U$=U$+" x 100":T%=2
1030 IF V>999 AND V<10000 THEN T%=3
1040 IF V>9999 THEN U$=U$+" x 10":T%=4
1050 IF V<10 THEN T%=0
1060 V=10*V/(10]T%)
1070 IF scale<>fsd THEN PROCscale:scale=fsd
1080 IF bezel$<>U$ THEN PROCbezel:bezel$=U$
1090 ENDPROC
```

THE DIGITAL DISPLAY

This is essentially the same program with the scale and
pointer part of the display replaced by a procedure to
print the reading on the screen in big letters. Once
listing 7.1 has been entered, it can be converted to a
digital display. Listing 7.2 shows the whole listing;
the main changes occur in PROCdisplay and PROCbiglet.
The latter procedure is similar to that used in listing
3.2. PROCdisplay converts the meter reading to a string
V$, which is then shortened to four characters long.
This is then printed on the screen using the big-letter
procedure. There is no need in this program for the
scale switch, as there is no scale.

```
 10 REM listing 7.2
 20 MODE1
 30 PROCinitialise
 40 REPEAT
 50 PROCdisplay
 60 UNTIL 0
 70 :
 80 DEFPROCinitialise
 90 @%=0:T%=2
100 bezel$=""
110 VDU23,255,0,126,126,126,126,126,126,0
120 VDU19,0,7,0,0,0
130 VDU19,1,4,0,0,0
```

```
140 VDU19,3,0,0,0,0
150 VDU23;8202;0;0;0;
160 ENDPROC
170 :
180 DEFPROCbezel
190 GCOL0,130
200 VDU24,0;0;1279;250;
210 CLG
220 GCOL0,3
230 X=640-(32*LEN(U$))
240 PROCdouble(U$,X,175)
250 VDU24,0;250;1279;1023;
260 ENDPROC
270 :
280 DEFPROCdisplay
290 PROCadval
300 COLOUR 1
310 V$=STR$(V/10)+"    "
320 V$=LEFT$(V$,4)
330 FOR n=1 TO 4
340 v$=MID$(V$,n,1)
350 PROCbiglet(v$,10*(n-1),10)
360 NEXT n
370 ENDPROC
380 :
390 DEFPROCdouble(A$,K,L)
400 LOCAL N
410 VDU5
420 A%=&A:X%=0:Y%=&A:D=&A00
430 FOR N=1 TO LEN(A$)
440 K1=K+(64*(N-1))
450 B$=MID$(A$,N,1)
460 ?D=ASC(B$)
470 CALL &FFF1
480 VDU23,240,D?1,D?1,D?2,D?2,D?3,D?3,D?4,D?4
490 VDU23,241,D?5,D?5,D?6,D?6,D?7,D?7,D?8,D?8
500 MOVE K1,L:PRINTCHR$(240);
510 MOVE K1,L-32:PRINTCHR$(241);
520 NEXT N
530 VDU4
540 ENDPROC
550 :
560 DEFPROCadval
570 V=0
580 FOR N=1 TO 100
590 V=V+ADVAL(1)/32
600 NEXT N
610 V=V*18/2048
620 I%=ADVAL(4) DIV32000
630 R%=ADVAL(2) DIV32000
640 IF R%>0 THEN V=V*10
650 IF I%>0 THEN U$="AMPERES" ELSE U$="VOLTS"
660 IF V<1000 THEN U$="MILLI"+U$
670 IF V>9 AND V<100 THEN U$=U$+" x 10":T%=1
680 IF V>99 AND V<1000 THEN U$=U$+" x 100":T%=2
690 IF V>999 AND V<10000 THEN T%=3
700 IF V>9999 THEN U$=U$+" x 10":T%=4
710 IF V<10 THEN T%=0
```

```
720 V=10*V/(10^T%)
730 IF bezel$<>U$ THEN PROCbezel:bezel$=U$
740 ENDPROC
750 :
760 DEFPROCbiglet(M$,X,Y)
770 M%=(6112+ASC(M$))*8
780 LOCAL H%,N%
790 FOR N%=0 TO 7
800 PRINTTAB(X,Y+N%);
810 FOR H%=0 TO 7
820 IF (N%?M% AND 2^(7-H%))>0 THEN VDU255 ELSE VDU32
830 NEXT H%,N%
840 ENDPROC
```

Appendix 1   A Program to Calculate Values

If all the theory given in chapter 1 is too much to cope with at once, and the idea of adding fractions is something that you thought was only ever done as a means of torture at school, then the following program will relieve the tedium of the mathematics. With practice, the maths is easy, but this program will handle most of the calculations required in the book. It can, of course, be extended to compute other formulae or, if an attractive display is unimportant, it can be shortened considerably. This program can also help to sort out the units. For example it is often difficult to work out whether the resistance is in ohms or Kohms.

The program will sum up to 10 resistances in series or in parallel, and will do the calculations involved with voltage dividers. It will work out the current given the voltage and resistance, or the current given the voltage and resistance, and it will also work out the power rating if the values of two out of the three variables (current, resistance and voltage) are entered.

```
 10 REM Listing APP1.1 Value calculator
 20 MODE 1
 30 ON ERROR GOTO60
 40 DIM val(10)
 50 REPEAT
 60 PROCinitialise
 70 PROCmenu
 80 UNTIL 0
 90 :
100 DEFPROCinitialise
110 res=0:@%=&30A
120 *FX11,0
130 R$=" k"+CHR$128
140 VDU4,20,26,15,12
150 VDU23,128,0,0,60,66,66,36,231,0
160 VDU23,1,0;0;0;0;
170 VDU19,0,4,0,0,0
180 PROCdouble("VALUE CALCULATOR",13,1,1)
190 VDU28,0,31,39,5
200 ENDPROC
```

```
210 :
220 DEFPROCmenu
230 PROCdouble("Options",17,0,2)
240 PRINT´"    1..Find series resistance"
250 PRINT´"    2..Find parallel resistance"
260 PRINT´"    3..Calculate voltage divider"
270 PRINT´"    4..Calculate voltage"
280 PRINT´"    5..Calculate current"
290 PRINT´"    6..Calculate power"
300 COLOUR 1
310 PRINT´´"    ESCAPE will return to this menu"
320 COLOUR 3
330 PRINT´´"    Enter a number";
340 optl=VAL(GET$)
350 CLS
360 IF optl=1 THEN PROCseries
370 IF optl=2 THEN PROCparallel
380 IF optl=3 THEN PROCdivider
390 IF optl=4 THEN PROCvoltage
400 IF optl=5 THEN PROCcurrent
410 IF optl=6 THEN PROCpower
420 ENDPROC
430 :
440 DEFPROCseries
450 PROCresistor
460 FOR T=1 TO number
470 res=res+val(T)
480 NEXT T
490 PRINT´´"Series resistance is ";res;R$
500 PROCspace
510 ENDPROC
520 :
530 DEFPROCparallel
540 PROCresistor
550 FOR T=1 TO number
560 IF val(T)=0 THEN GOTO 590
570 res=res*val(T)/(res+val(T))
580 IF res=0 THEN res=val(T)
590 NEXT T
600 PRINT´´"Parallel resistance is ";res;R$
610 PROCspace
620 ENDPROC
630 :
640 DEFPROCresistor
650 IF optl=1 THEN
    PROCdouble("Series resistance",13,0,2)
660 IF optl=2 THEN
    PROCdouble("Parallel resistance",12,0,2)
670 REPEAT
680 INPUT´´"How many resistors "number
690 UNTIL number<10 AND number>1
700 COLOUR 2
710 PRINT´"Enter values in"R$´
720 COLOUR 3
730 FOR T=1 TO number
740 PRINT"Value for resistor·";T;" ";
750 INPUT val(T)
760 NEXT T
```

```
 770 ENDPROC
 780 :
 790 DEFPROCdivider
 800 PROCdouble("Voltage divider",13,0,2)
 810 PRINT'"1...1 known resistance"
 820 PRINT'"2...Ratio for unknown resistances"
 830 PRINT'"3...Value for unknown resistances"
 840 PRINT'"4...Calculate voltage"
 850 PRINT''"Enter a number"
 860 REPEAT opt2=VAL(GET$)
 870 UNTIL opt2>0 AND opt2<6
 880 CLS
 890 PROCdouble("Voltage divider",13,0,2)
 900 PROCdiagram
 910 MOVE 384,736
 920 INPUT"Enter input voltage "vmax
 930 GCOL0,1
 940 MOVE 16,800
 950 PRINT;vmax"v"
 960 GCOL0,3
 970 IF opt2=1 THEN PROCdiv1
 980 IF opt2=2 THEN PROCdiv2
 990 IF opt2=3 THEN PROCdiv3
1000 IF opt2=4 THEN PROCdiv4
1010 PROCspace
1020 ENDPROC
1030 :
1040 DEFPROCdiv1
1050 PROCvout
1060 MOVE 384,608
1070 PRINT"Enter resistance in"R$;
1080 INPUT" "res
1090 MOVE 384,546
1100 INPUT"Is this resistor A or B",A$
1110 IF A$<>"A" THEN A$="B"
1120 IF A$="A" THEN PROCa(res):
     PROCb(res*vout/(vmax-vout))
1130 IF A$="B" THEN PROCb(res):
     PROCa(res*(vmax-vout)/vout)
1140 ENDPROC
1150 :
1160 DEFPROCdiv2
1170 PROCvout
1180 MOVE384,608
1190 PRINT"Ratio A:B = 1:";vout/(vmax-vout)
1200 MOVE384,546
1210 PRINT"Ratio B:A = 1:";(vmax-vout)/vout
1220 ENDPROC
1230 :
1240 DEFPROCdiv3
1250 PROCvout
1260 MOVE 384,608
1270 INPUT"Enter current (ma) "amp
1280 PROCa((vmax-vout)/amp)
1290 PROCb(vout/amp)
1300 ENDPROC
1310 :
1320 DEFPROCdiv4
```

```
1330 MOVE 384,672
1340 PRINT"Enter resistance A in"R$;
1350 INPUT" "resA
1360 PROCa(resA)
1370 MOVE 384,608
1380 PRINT"Enter resistance B in"R$;
1390 INPUT" "resB
1400 PROCb(resB)
1410 vout=resB*(vmax/(resA+resB))
1420 PROCprintvout
1430 ENDPROC
1440 :
1450 DEFPROCvoltage
1460 PROCdouble("Calculate voltage",13,0,2)
1470 INPUT´´´"Enter current in milliamps "amp
1480 PRINT´"Enter resistance in "R$;
1490 INPUT" "res
1500 COLOUR 2
1510 PRINT´´"Voltage = ";(amp*res);" volts"
1520 PROCspace
1530 ENDPROC
1540 :
1550 DEFPROCcurrent
1560 PROCdouble("Calculate current",13,0,2)
1570 INPUT´´´"Enter voltage "volt
1580 PRINT´"Enter resistance in "R$;
1590 INPUT" "res
1600 COLOUR 2
1610 PRINT´´"Current = ";(volt/res);" milliamps"
1620 PROCspace
1630 ENDPROC
1640 :
1650 DEFPROCpower
1660 PROCdouble("Calculate power rating",10,0,2)
1670 LOCAL volt,amp,res,power
1680 PRINT´"  1...Voltage"
1690 PRINT´"  2...Current"
1700 PRINT´"  3...Resistance"
1710 PRINT´´"  Select a parameter"´
1720 opt3=VAL(GET$)
1730 IF opt3=1 THEN INPUT"  Enter voltage "volt
1740 IF opt3=2 THEN INPUT
     "  Enter current in milliamps "amp :amp=amp/1000
1750 IF opt3=3 THEN PRINT"  Enter resistance in"R$;:
     INPUT" "res:res=res*1000
1760 IF volt=0 THEN power=amp*amp*res
1770 IF amp=0 AND res>0 THEN power=volt*volt/res
1780 IF res=0 THEN power=volt*amp
1790 IF power=0 THEN GOTO 1710
1800 COLOUR 2
1810 PRINT´"  Power rating = ";power;" watts"´´
1820 PROCspace
1830 ENDPROC
1840 :
1850 DEFPROCdouble(P$,X,Y,col)
1860 COLOUR col
1870 A%=10:X%=0:Y%=10:p=&A00
```

```
1880 FOR N=1 TO LENP$
1890 p$=MID$(P$,N,1)
1900 ?p=ASCp$:CALL&FFF1
1910 VDU23,240,p?1,p?1,p?2,p?2,p?3,p?3,p?4,p?4
1920 VDU23,241,p?5,p?5,p?6,p?6,p?7,p?7,p?8,p?8
1930 PRINTTAB(X+N-1,Y)CHR$240
1940 PRINTTAB(X+N-1,Y+1)CHR$241
1950 NEXT N
1960 COLOUR 3
1970 ENDPROC
1980 :
1990 DEFPROCspace
2000 VDU24,175;10;1100;60;5,18,0,131,12,18,0,0
2010 MOVE200,47:PRINT"Press space bar to continue"
2020 *FX15,0
2030 REPEAT:UNTIL GET=32
2040 VDU4,18,0,128,16,18,0,3,26,28,1,6,38,1,12
2050 ENDPROC
2060 :
2070 DEFPROCdiagram
2080 VDU5
2090 FOR N=0 TO 96 STEP 16
2100 MOVE 32+N,96
2110 DRAW 48+N,128
2120 NEXT N
2130 DRAW 32,128
2140 MOVE 16,608:PRINT"A"
2150 MOVE 16,320:PRINT"B"
2160 MOVE 80,128:DRAW 80,224
2170 FOR N=224 TO 512 STEP 288
2180 MOVE 64,N:DRAW 96,N
2190 DRAW 96,N+192
2200 DRAW 64,N+192
2210 DRAW 64,N
2220 NEXT N
2230 MOVE 80,704:DRAW 80,768
2240 MOVE 80,416:DRAW 80,512
2250 MOVE 48,768:DRAW 112,768
2260 MOVE 80,464:DRAW 160,464
2270 MOVE 144,448:DRAW 160,464
2280 DRAW 144,480
2290 ENDPROC
2300 :
2310 DEFPROCa(r)
2320 GCOL0,2
2330 MOVE 128,648:PRINT;r
2340 MOVE 96,586:PRINTR$
2350 GCOL0,3
2360 ENDPROC
2370 :
2380 DEFPROCb(r)
2390 GCOL0,2
2400 MOVE 128,360:PRINT;r
2410 MOVE 96,296:PRINTR$
2420 GCOL0,3
2430 ENDPROC
2440 :
2450 DEFPROCprintvout
```

```
2460 GCOL0,1
2470 MOVE 160,508:PRINT;vout
2480 MOVE 160,440:PRINT"v"
2490 GCOL0,3
2500 ENDPROC
2510 :
2520 DEFPROCvout
2530 MOVE 384,672
2540 INPUT"Enter output voltage "vout
2550 REM Ensure that volts out is
2560 REM always less than volts in.
2570 IF vout>=vmax THEN vout=vmax-0.0000001
2580 PROCprintvout
2590 ENDPROC
```

Description of Program

PROCinitialise sets up all the variables required by the program, defines the ohms symbol, switches off the cursor and changes the background colour to blue. Once the title has been printed a text window is created so that clearing the screen will leave the title on the screen. The print format is set by @% to give three places of decimals. Given the inaccuracies inherent in the measurements and components, this order of accuracy is quite sufficient.

PROCmenu is the menu selection procedure. If a number outside the range 1 to 6 is entered, control returns to the infinite REPEAT...UNTIL loop at lines 50-80, and the program restarts.

PROCseries calculates the series resistance and prints it out.

PROCparallel calculates the parallel resistance and prints it out.

PROCresistor is the common element of PROCseries and PROCparallel. It asks for the number of resistors to be summed, checks that the value is within a sensible range, and then asks for the value of each. The values are stored in the array ´val´.

PROCdivider presents a menu from which to select the option. After printing the title and drawing the circuit diagram (PROCdiagram), the input voltage is entered and displayed on the diagram.

PROCdivl is the option to calculate the unknown resistance, given a known resistance and the output voltage. The values are displayed on the circuit diagram.

PROCdiv2 is the option to calculate the ratio of the two resistors once the output voltage has been entered.

PROCdiv3 is the option to print out the resistances, given the output voltage and the current. These are displayed on the diagram.

PROCdiv4 is the option to print the output voltage given the resistances and the current.

PROCvoltage calculates the voltage, given the current and resistance.

PROCcurrent calculates the current, given the voltage and resistance.

PROCpower calculates the power rating. The procedure is so designed that any two of the three parameters can be entered in any order.

PROCdouble is a useful routine to print double height in modes 0 to 6. CALL&FFF1 with A%=10 is an OSWORD call to read a character definition and X and Y give the memory location (in this case &A00) where the ASCII code of the character is first put, then where the OSWORD routine will store the 8 parameters that define the character. See the chapter on Assembler Language in the User Guide for more details of the OSWORD call.

PROCspace is a routine to wait until the space bar is pressed. The message is printed in reverse colours at the bottom of the screen. The complicated VDU statements need to be entered carefully if mistakes are to be avoided. They program a graphics window, change colours, and return things to normal at the end of the procedure. Line 140 has been inserted in PROCinitialise to restore things should ESCAPE be pressed while in this procedure.

PROCdiagram draws the circuit diagram of the voltage divider network.

PROCa prints the value of resistor A on the circuit diagram.

PROCb prints the value of resistor B on the circuit diagram.

PROCprintvout prints the output voltage on the circuit diagram.

PROCvout is the procedure to input the value of the output voltage. If a value is entered that is higher than the input voltage, the output voltage is made fractionally smaller than the input voltage. In practice, in such a circuit the output voltage could not exceed the input voltage. The reason for making it just slightly smaller is to prevent 'Division by zero' errors in some of the calculations. The fraction is so small as to make very little difference to the final values.

Appendix 2   Resistor Colour Code Program

This program is designed to help the reader become familiar with resistor colour codes. These are easy to decipher with practice, and what better is there than to use the computer for that practice! This program posed one or two problems: for instance, how does one get orange, brown or grey colours on the screen? If mode 2 is used, there are 8 colours available (not counting the flashing colours). Most of the resistor colour codes are the same as these 8 colours, but the other colours can be made by using colour-mixing techniques. To make orange, if alternate red and yellow dots are placed on the screen, then the colour will appear orange. This technique works better in mode 1 where the dot size is smaller, but mode 2 must be used in this application because it is the only mode that offers the 8 colours. The easiest way to put alternate dots of colour on the screen is to program two user-defined characters as opposite sets of alternate dots. Then if the text and graphics cursors are combined using VDU5, the second character can be overprinted on the first in a different colour. In this program, the two characters programmed are CHR$129 and CHR$130 (figure A2.1).

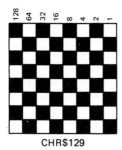
CHR$129

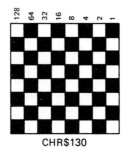
CHR$130

Figure A2.1

The colours are not perfect, but they can be identified quite readily. In practice, the colour bands on resistors are not always clearly marked and it is sometimes difficult to tell, say, the brown from the orange.

The second problem that makes the program less straightforward than might at first appear is the differing systems of notation for the resistor value. Apart from the obvious value which is stored as an integer in variable R%, the resistor value needs to be stored in ´colour code´ notation. This is a four or five figure number which is stored in string variable B$ and each number is the colour number of the appropriate band on the resistor (excluding the tolerance band). Finally the value needs to be stored in the notation in which it is entered into the computer. This notation is the way the resistor value is normally written. This is stored in two parts. The numeric part is stored in variable R and the ´K´ or ´M´ and the ´Ω´ are stored in string variable R$. As the numeric variable can have a fractional part it cannot be stored in an integer variable. The ´Ω´ sign does not need to be entered; this is inserted when the RETURN key is pressed. The 3 values are stored as follows

```
      resistor value 4.7K
      R% .. 4700
      B$ .. 472
      R  .. 4.7      R$  .. K
```

The program allows either 4 band or 5 band codes to be selected in the 12 ´preferred´ values for each decade or in the extended range of 24 values. It will give a random selection of values from 10 ohms up to 9.1 Mohms. The user has the option of seeing as many examples as required before a test is given. The test asks 10 questions, and there are two opportunities to get the right answer. 5 points are given for an answer that is correct at the first attempt, and 2 points if it is correct at the second attempt. After an incorrect second attempt, the answer is displayed. The answers must be given in the same format as that in which they are printed in the demonstration part of the program - for example 4.7KΩ.

```
10 REM Listing A2.1 Resistor codes
20 MODE 2
30 DIM col1(9),col2(9),series(24)
40 PROCinitialise
50 PROCdraw_resistor
60 REPEAT
70 PROCreset
```

```
 80 PROCmenu
 90 UNTIL 0
100 END
110 :
120 DEFPROCinitialise
130 *FX11,0
140 COLOUR 3
150 PRINTTAB(6,1)"RESISTOR"
160 PRINTTAB(4,3)"COLOUR CODES"
170 COLOUR 7
180 VDU23,128,255,255,255,255,255,255,255,255
190 VDU23,129,170,85,170,85,170,85,170,85
200 VDU23,130,85,170,85,170,85,170,85,170
210 VDU23,131,0,0,60,66,66,36,231,0
220 FOR N=0 TO 9
230 READ col1(N),col2(N)
240 NEXT N
250 FOR N=1 TO 24
260 READ series(N)
270 NEXT N
280 DATA 0,0,2,1,1,1,1,3,3,3
290 DATA 2,2,4,4,5,4,7,0,7,7
300 DATA 10,12,15,18,22,27,33,39,47,56,68,82
310 DATA 11,13,16,20,24,30,36,43,51,62,75,91
320 ENDPROC
330 :
340 DEFPROCdraw_resistor
350 MOVE 188,604:DRAW 1092,604
360 DRAW 1092,800:DRAW 188,800
370 DRAW 188,604
380 FOR N=0 TO 8 STEP 4
390 Y=696+N
400 MOVE 32,Y:DRAW 188,Y
410 MOVE 1092,Y:DRAW 1247,Y
420 NEXT N
430 MOVE 320,600:DRAW 184,600
440 DRAW 184,804:DRAW 320,804
450 MOVE 320,596:DRAW 180,596
460 DRAW 180,808:DRAW 320,808
470 MOVE 960,600:DRAW 1096,600
480 DRAW 1096,804:DRAW 960,804
490 MOVE 960,596:DRAW 1100,596
500 DRAW 1100,808:DRAW 960,808
510 ENDPROC
520 :
530 DEFPROCreset
540 VDU26,5
550 FOR N=0 TO 13
560 FOR T=0 TO 5
570 GCOL0,5
580 MOVE 192+64*N,636+32*T
590 PRINTCHR$129
600 GCOL0,3
610 MOVE 192+64*N,636+32*T
620 PRINTCHR$130
630 NEXT T,N
640 FOR T=0 TO 5
650 GCOL 0,1
```

```
 660 MOVE 960,636+32*T
 670 PRINTCHR$128
 680 NEXT T
 690 VDU4,28,0,31,19,15,12
 700 VDU23,1,0;0;0;0;
 710 ENDPROC
 720 :
 730 DEFPROCdraw_bands
 740 VDU5
 750 FOR N= 1 TO B%-1
 760 val=VAL(MID$(B$,N,1))
 770 FOR Y=636   TO 796 STEP 32
 780 GCOL 0,col1(val)
 790 MOVE 128+128*N,Y
 800 PRINTCHR$129
 810 GCOL 0,col2(val)
 820 MOVE 128+128*N,Y
 830 PRINTCHR$130
 840 NEXT Y
 850 NEXT N
 860 VDU4,23,1,0;0;0;0;
 870 ENDPROC
 880 :
 890 DEFPROCmenu
 900 PRINT´"1. normal range"
 910 PRINT´"2. extended range"
 920 PRINT´´"Enter number"
 930 A%=12
 940 a$=GET$
 950 IF a$="2" THEN A%=24
 960 CLS
 970 COLOUR 1
 980 PRINTTAB(3,1)"select  option"
 990 COLOUR 7
1000 PRINT´´"1. 4 band examples"
1010 PRINT´´"2. 5 band examples"
1020 PRINT´´"3. 4 band test"
1030 PRINT´´"4. 5 band test"
1040 PRINT´´"Enter 1-4";
1050 option=VAL(GET$)
1060 CLS
1070 IF option=1 THEN B%=4:PROCdemo
1080 IF option=2 THEN B%=5:PROCdemo
1090 IF option=3 THEN B%=4:PROCtest
1100 IF option=4 THEN B%=5:PROCtest
1110 ENDPROC
1120 :
1130 DEFPROCdemo
1140 REPEAT
1150 PROCencode
1160 PROCdraw_bands
1170 PRINT´´"Value is ";R;R$
1180 COLOUR 1
1190 PRINT´´´"Press space bar to"
1200 PRINT´"continue, E to end"
1210 COLOUR 7
1220 A$=GET$
1230 CLS
```

```
1240 UNTIL A$="E"
1250 ENDPROC
1260 :
1270 DEFPROCencode
1280 oldR%=R%
1290 REPEAT
1300 R%=series(RND(A%))*10^(RND(5))
1310 UNTIL R%<>oldR%
1320 val$=STR$(R%):R$=""
1330 FOR N=1 TO B%-2
1340 R$=R$+LEFT$(val$,1)
1350 val$=MID$(val$,2)
1360 NEXT N
1370 B$=R$+STR$(LEN(val$))
1380 R=R%:R$=""
1390 IF R>999999 THEN R=R/1000000:R$="M"
1400 IF R>999 THEN R=R/1000:R$="K"
1410 R$=R$+CHR$131
1420 ENDPROC
1430 :
1440 DEFPROCtest
1450 flag=0:total=0
1460 FOR Q=1 TO 10
1470 PROCencode
1480 PROCdraw_bands
1490 testval=R:testval$=R$
1500 REPEAT
1510 CLS
1520 PRINT"Question ";Q;
1530 IF flag=1 THEN PRINT" 2nd try";
1540 PRINT´´"Enter value ";
1550 PROCinput
1560 IF testval=R AND testval$=R$ THEN PROCright:
     ELSE PROCwrong
1570 UNTIL flag=0
1580 PRINTTAB(0,12)"Score = ";total
1590 i=INKEY(400)
1600 NEXT Q
1610 PRINT´"Press space bar"
1620 REPEAT:UNTIL GET=32
1630 ENDPROC
1640 :
1650 DEFPROCright
1660 COLOUR 5
1670 PRINT´´"CORRECT"
1680 SOUND 1,-15,125,5
1690 COLOUR 7
1700 IF flag=0 THEN score = 5 ELSE score=2
1710 total=total+score
1720 flag=0
1730 ENDPROC
1740 :
1750 DEFPROCwrong
1760 COLOUR 6
1770 PRINT´"WRONG"´
1780 SOUND 1,-15,25,5
1790 COLOUR 7
1800 IF flag=0 THEN PRINT"Try again":flag=1:GOTO1840
```

```
1810 PRINT"The value was ";testval;testval$
1820 COLOUR 7
1830 flag=0
1840 PRINT'"Press space bar"
1850 REPEAT:UNTIL GET=32
1860 ENDPROC
1870 :
1880 DEFPROCinput
1890 a$="":A$="":R$=""
1900 REPEAT
1910 REPEAT
1920 A$=A$+a$
1930 PRINTa$;
1940 a$=GET$
1950 IF a$=CHR$(127) THEN PROCdelete
1960 UNTIL a$<"0" OR a$>"9"
1970 R=VAL(A$)
1980 IF a$>"9" THEN R$=a$
1990 UNTIL a$=CHR$(13)
2000 R$=R$+CHR$131:PRINTCHR$131
2010 ENDPROC
2020 :
2030 DEFPROCdelete
2040 a$=""
2050 PRINTCHR$127;
2060 A$=LEFT$(A$,LEN(A$-1))
2070 ENDPROC
```

Description of Program

Lines 20-100 are the main part of the program, with control being given to the various procedures described below. Line 30 dimensions 3 arrays: ´col1´ and ´col2´ store the numbers for the alternate colours for the colour mixing. To keep the routine to draw the bands simple, the single-coloured bands are constructed as described above, except that both colours are the same. The array ´series´ holds all the preferred resistor values. The main run-loop of the program is an infinite REPEAT...UNTIL loop, calling up PROCreset and PROCmenu.

PROCinitialise sets up all the variables needed for the program. It switches off the auto-key repeat, prints the program title and defines four user-defined characters, the two mentioned above, a full block, and the Ω symbol. The appropriate values are stored in the arrays, ready for use later in the program.

PROCdraw_resistor draws the outline of the resistor on the screen. This does not need to be frequently redrawn, as PROC reset will clear the inside of it.

PROCreset fills the inside of the resistor with a pink colour using the colour mixing technique. Pink was chosen because all the colour bands stand out well against it. Do not forget that there is a black band! This procedure also draws a red band on the right to represent the tolerance band. Because of the colours involved it is somewhat more difficult to provide an exercise on this, and besides, one tends to buy resistors all with the same tolerance.

PROCdraw_bands draws the colour bands on the resistor. B% is the number of bands and will have a value of either 4 or 5. At the end of the procedure when the normal text and graphics cursors are restored, the cursor is switched off.

PROCmenu presents the various options for the user. A% is the number of resistor values per decade, and takes the value of 12 or 24. The default value is set to 12; this avoids the need for having a checking routine, which would otherwise be necessary to test whether or not the correct keys have been pressed. This procedure then calls up either the demonstration or the test.

PROCdemo first selects a resistor value using PROCencode, then draws the bands and prints the value on the screen. This procedure will carry on until ´E´ is pressed.

PROCencode first selects a resistor value at random. It checks to make sure it was not the same as the previous one (very annoying when the same question comes up twice running!). It then puts the value into the formats described above, which simplifies the other procedures.

PROCtest is very similar to PROCdemo except that the value has to be input. Command passes to PROCright or PROCwrong, depending on the answer. The variable ´flag´ is used to show whether an attempt at the answer has already been made.

PROCright is the procedure to make a bleep and increase the score if the right answer is entered.

PROCwrong is the procedure that control passes to if the answer is wrong. The action taken depends on whether or not ´flag´ has been set by a previous incorrect answer.

PROCinput is a routine to input one character at a time for the answer. This routine has been made necessary by the different notations used for the resistor value.

PROCdelete is the routine to remove a character should the delete key be pressed.

Appendix 3   User Port Board Designer

The following program greatly simplifies the design of circuit boards for use with the User Port. It allows board layouts to be designed and displayed on the computer screen and easily changed. The cursor keys are used to move the cursor around the screen, and the appropriate key is then pressed to start the drawing of the component. When the component is positioned correctly, it can be ´fixed´ in position by pressing the space bar. It first draws the board layout, 34 tracks wide, having allowed the user to make the board from 10 up to 40 holes high. The input plug is drawn and the output socket will also be drawn if required. It will draw yellow rectangles to represent integrated circuits or other large components, resistors in white (mounting them vertically if the space is too small), other small components in red, links in cyan, and track cuts in green. If a component has been placed incorrectly, it can be ´undrawn´ by going over the component again. At the end of the program is a procedure that can be included to dump the layout to a printer. As there is such a wide variety of printers available, no dump routine has actually been included in the program, but two are included here for the common printers. Other printers often have very similar commands to these, so it would be possible to adapt one of these programs to suit most printers. It should be noted that for either of these routines, if the printer does not have line feed set, the VDU1,10 command must be changed to read VDU1,10,1,13.

Acorn/Seikosha GP80/GP100 printers

```
1500 DEFPROCdump
1510 VDU2,1,8
1520 FOR Y%=1023 TO 111 STEP-28
1530 FOR X%=0 TO 1277 STEP3:D%=0
1540 FOR y%=27 TO 0 STEP-4:D%=D%*2
1550 IF POINT(X%,Y%-y%)>0 D%=D%+1
1560 NEXT y%:VDU1,D%+128
1570 NEXT X%:VDU1,10
1580 NEXT Y%:VDU1,15,3
1590 ENDPROC
```

Epson MX80,RX80,FX80 printers

```
1500 DEFPROCdump
1510 VDU2,1,27,1,51,1,24
1520 FOR Y% = 1023 TO 127 STEP-16
1530 VDU2,1,27,1,75,1,170,1,1
1540 FOR X% = 0 TO 1277 STEP3:D%=0
1550 FOR y%=0 TO 7:D%=D%*2
1560 IF POINT(X%,Y%-y%*2)>0 D%=D%+1
1570 NEXT y%:VDU1,D%:NEXT X%
1580 VDU1,10:NEXT Y%:VDU3
1590 ENDPROC
```

Function key 0 has been defined so that if the program has typing errors in it, or if it is wished to extend the facilities of the program, then pressing function key 0 will list the program in mode 7. The operation of the cursor keys is then restored to normal, and page mode is put on. Function key 0 will, of course, work only when the program has stopped running, or after ESCAPE has been pressed.

The program has been written to fit in with the sort of board designs that are needed to build your own extra User and Analogue Port applications, and therefore it is somewhat limited in its scope of use. The program could be altered and extended to enable extra features to be included in order to make it more versatile.

```
 10 REM Listing A3.1 Board designer
 20 MODE 1
 30 PROCscreen
 40 MODE2
 50 PROCinitialise
 60 PROCgrid
 70 PROCplug
 80 IF INSTR("Yy",A$)>0 THEN PROCsocket
 90 PROCinput
100 END
110 :
120 DEFPROCinitialise
130 *KEY0 OLD¦M MODE7¦M *FX4,0¦M ¦N LIST¦M
140 VDU23,240,0,16,16,16,124,16,16,16
150 VDU23,241,0,0,40,16,16,16,40,0
160 VDU23,242,16,56,124,124,124,124,56,16
170 FOR N=0 TO 7
180 VDU19,8+N,N,0,0,0
190 NEXT N
200 ENDPROC
210 :
220 DEFPROCscreen
230 VDU19,0,4,0,0,0
240 COLOUR 1
```

```
250 *FX4,1
260 PRINTTAB(10,1)"CIRCUIT BOARD DESIGNER"
270 COLOUR 2
280 PRINTTAB(12,4)"L...Draw link"
290 PRINTTAB(12,6)"I...Draw IC"
300 PRINTTAB(12,8)"C...Draw component"
310 PRINTTAB(12,10)"X...Cut track"
320 PRINTTAB(12,12)"R...Draw resistor"
330 PRINTTAB(12,14)"P...Printout"
340 COLOUR 3
350 PRINTTAB(9,17)"Press space to finish,"
360 PRINTTAB(9,18)"use cursor keys to move"
370 COLOUR 1
380 PRINTTAB(12,20)SPC(18)
390 INPUTTAB(12,20)"How many rows "row
400 IF row>40 OR row<10 THEN GOTO 380
410 PRINTTAB(6,22)"Do you want an O/P socket";
420 A$=GET$
430 ENDPROC
440 :
450 DEFPROCgrid
460 FOR X=40 TO 1096 STEP 32
470 FOR Y=40 TO (16+row*24) STEP 24
480 IF X*Y MOD5=0 THEN GCOL0,2 ELSE GCOL0,7
490 PLOT 69,X,Y
500 NEXT Y,X
510 ENDPROC
520 :
530 DEFPROCplug
540 GCOL0,3
550 FOR N=0 TO 11
560 MOVE 392+N*32,0
570 DRAW 392+N*32,64
580 NEXT N
590 GCOL0,4
600 FOR N=0 TO 3
610 MOVE 392,40+4*N
620 DRAW 744,40+4*N
630 NEXT N
640 ENDPROC
650 :
660 DEFPROCsocket
670 Y=16+row*24
680 GCOL0,3:MOVE 376,Y-72
690 DRAW 760,Y-72:DRAW 760,Y
700 DRAW 376,Y:DRAW 376,Y-72
710 ENDPROC
720 :
730 DEFPROCinput
740 VDU5:X=40:Y=40
750 REPEAT
760 GCOL3,6:MOVE X-24,Y+16
770 VDU240:x=X:y=Y:PROCmove
780 MOVE x-24,y+16:VDU240
790 IF A=67 THEN VDU7:PROCline(1):PROCcomp(1)
800 IF A=73 THEN VDU7:PROCic
810 IF A=76 THEN VDU7:PROCline(5)
820 IF A=80 THEN VDU7:PROCdump
```

```
830 IF A=82 THEN VDU7:PROCresistor
840 IF A=88 THEN VDU7,18,3,2,25,4,X-24;Y+16;241
850 UNTIL 0
860 ENDPROC
870 :
880 DEFPROCic
890 GCOL3,3
900 REPEAT
910 X1=X:Y1=Y
920 PROCrect(x,y,X1,Y1)
930 PROCmove
940 PROCrect(x,y,X1,Y1)
950 UNTIL A=32:VDU7
960 PROCrect(x,y,X,Y)
970 ENDPROC
980 :
990 DEFPROCline(col)
1000 GCOL3,col
1010 REPEAT
1020 X1=X:Y1=Y
1030 MOVE x,y:PLOT 6,X1,Y1
1040 PROCmove:MOVE x,y
1050 PLOT 6,X1,Y1
1060 UNTIL A=32:VDU7
1070 MOVE x,y:DRAW X,Y
1080 ENDPROC
1090 :
1100 DEFPROCresistor
1110 PROCline(7)
1120 IF x=X AND y=Y THEN ENDPROC
1130 IFx=X GOTO 1210
1140 IFy=Y GOTO 1150 ELSE PROCcomp(7):ENDPROC
1150 X1=(X-x)/2+x
1160 IF ABS(X-x)<128 THEN PROCcomp(7):ENDPROC
1170 FOR N=-12 TO 12 STEP 4
1180 MOVE X1-32,Y+N:DRAW X1+32,Y+N
1190 NEXT N
1200 GOTO1260
1210 Y1=(Y-y)/2+y
1220 IF ABS(Y-y)<128 THEN PROCcomp(7):ENDPROC
1230 FOR N=-16 TO 16 STEP 8
1240 MOVE X+N,Y1-24:DRAW X+N,Y1+24
1250 NEXT N
1260 ENDPROC
1270 :
1280 DEFPROCmove
1290 A=GET
1300 IF A=136 AND X>63 THEN X=X-32
1310 IF A=137 AND X<1079 THEN X=X+32
1320 IF A=138 AND Y>56 THEN Y=Y-24
1330 IF A=139 AND Y<(16+row*24) THEN Y=Y+24
1340 ENDPROC
1350 :
1360 DEFPROCrect(x1,y1,x2,y2)
1370 IFx2<x1 THEN x3=x1:x1=x2:x2=x3
1380 IFy2<y1 THEN y3=y1:y1=y2:y2=y3
1390 MOVE x1-16,y1-12:DRAW x1-16,y2+12
1400 DRAW x2+16,y2+12:DRAW x2+16,y1-12
```

```
1410 DRAW x1-16,y1-12
1420 ENDPROC
1430 :
1440 DEFPROCcomp(col)
1450 GCOL3,col
1460 MOVE x-24,y+16
1470 VDU242
1480 ENDPROC
1490 :
1500 DEFPROCdump
1510 REM *************************
1520 REM *                       *
1530 REM *                       *
1540 REM * Put print dump routine *
1550 REM *           here        *
1560 REM *                       *
1570 REM *                       *
1580 REM *************************
1590 ENDPROC
```

Index